B. C.

Let God Go Free

BY ERNEST HARRISON

THE SEABURY PRESS

NEW YORK

PRINTED AND BOUND IN CANADA

The Christian Church is passing through a prolonged crisis. Much criticism is being declared, most of it from the members themselves.

The following book accepts this criticism gladly and suggests ways in which we can use it to make new discoveries about God.

To

HELEN MILTON

who suggested the title and much of the background.

CONTENTS

CHAPTER ONE

LEARNING TO LIVE

When I was a child, I thought everyone loved me. This was the belief on which my world was built, and everything I did reflected it. Then one day I overheard two adults discussing me, and there was no mistaking their meaning. They disliked me intensely.

My whole world was shattered. If two people who appeared to find me attractive actually despised me, what about the rest? After an unhappy night of heavy tears and punched pillows, I ran to a favorite uncle, who slowly untangled the mess.

'No two people are going to look at you in the same way,' he said, 'and you may as well adjust to it. We're all in the same boat. A few like us; a few dislike us; and the majority are neutral.'

I don't know whether these were his exact words, but that is how I remember them, and they saved me from disaster. Something had happened which challenged me to change some (not all) of my existing assumptions and he had shown me how to do it.

Looking back, I can see that there were other, less satisfactory, solutions which I might have grasped in my misery. I might, for example, have pretended that the incident had not taken place or that the two I had overheard were really exceptions. I could then have taken care that such an incident never occurred again and, in course of time, convinced myself that my first beliefs had been right: that I was in fact loved by everyone.

Alternatively, I might have persuaded myself (or my uncle might have persuaded me) that the people I overheard were really unpleasant, wicked people, and that any right minded person would completely ignore what they said. I had thought that everyone loved me and so it remained. Everyone *did* love me—everyone who was good, that is. Not unchristian people like those others. Once again, my escape from the challenge would have been complete. For, if I only listened to those who agreed with me, and wrote off those

1

who disagreed, then I would be safe from any unpleasant discoveries concerning myself and free from having to change.

Or I might have tried a more subtle escape from the problem by falling into a mood of deep despair. On the face of it, this would have appeared as a great change, a move from one extreme to the other. But such a move would have been deceptive. What looked like change would only have been an excuse to keep myself safe. There is great pleasure, as I found out during that tearful night, in self pity. 'Nobody loves me' is as deep a luxury as 'everybody loves me'. By deciding that nobody in his right mind could possibly love me, I would have protected myself against any further hurt because, whenever I overheard a conversation like the one which had first upset me, I would be able to say—'Of course, I knew I was no good.' And so, in spite of outward appearances, I would not have adjusted to the new discovery at all. I would simply have ignored it by pretending that it displaced everything I had previously believed.

Such incidents occur in everyone's life. The details vary, of course, as do the solutions; but every person experiences moments when it seems as if everything is being challenged and even undermined. He wishes that the ground would swallow him up or that he had never been born. He would like to shout, in the words of a Broadway musical: *Stop the world, I want to get off.* A simple existence has suddenly become complex, a gay one sad, a faithful one riddled with doubt.

In general terms, he can adopt any of the four solutions mentioned above: he can accept the challenge, look at its good features, look at the bad, and try to make such changes as seem necessary; or he can shut his ears to it and pretend it does not exist; or he can say that it is wicked and should not be allowed to undermine the old, right ideas; or he can fall into despair and conclude that the old ideas were altogether wrong.

What is true of the individual is also true of the Church. As the centuries have passed, discoveries have come along which have challenged Christians to alter their ideas, sometimes radically. Yet, only on rare occasions has the Church been willing to question freely its established notions or customs. More often, it has first of all pretended that there was no problem and then, forced to acknowledge its presence, denounced those who posed the problems as evil.

We are living in an age when there are challenges in every area of our lives, and the Church is not exempt from any of them. Nor is any part of the Church's work left unscathed. We are called upon to change our beliefs about God, our ideas about prayer and worship, the nature of the Church, the principles of morality, the meaning of Mission, the uniqueness of Christianity, and so on. We are challenged to examine with the greatest of care and the minimum of prejudice our creeds, our sacraments, and our ministry.

What is our response to be? We can, of course, pretend that there is no problem: the Faith which was 'once for all delivered to the saints' came in a gift-wrapped package, neat and unchangeable. Or we can declare that those who criticize are wicked, that the Bishop of Woolwich has no right to be a bishop, and that the clergy who write these critical books have broken their ordination vows. Or we can pretend to change by going to the other extreme: by saying that the Church is beyond redemption, a society of self-willed fools who will help the world most by voting for their own dissolution.

The fourth response is the one implied in the following chapters: that we look at the challenges carefully, asking ourselves where they seem right and where they do not. Every suggestion of change is not a good one. For every Einstein who took the right turning, there are a thousand scientists who took the wrong one. All that is asked here is that we accept, without fear, the equally valid statement that, for every *Christian* who took the right turning, there are a thousand who took the wrong one. Every suggestion of change is not a bad one.

This book will concern itself with certain areas of life which many Christians have clearly identified as among those in which the Church is called upon for great and sometimes radical reform. If we do not make these reforms we shall, if I hear the warnings of our present-day prophets, fail and pass into a deserved oblivion.

The reforms which I have selected for examination fall into a pattern. My purpose throughout the book is to indicate parts of our religious life in which we have tried to imprison God. In our anxiety to be secure and certain in our relationships with him, we have tried, and still try, to bring him into a tight focus which will reveal to us precisely and exactly where he is, what he is declaring, when he is pleased, and when he is angry. The effort has never proved successful, but we never give up trying.

In his earliest days, man used physical boxes in which he could trap God—trees, waterfalls, mountains, plots of ground, churches and temples. As he became more sophisticated, so did his prisons. Attempts were made to bring God within our power by the use of certain men, such as patriarchs, in whom he was thought to dwell more than in the rest of us. Then Laws were used, Religions, Creeds, Doctrines, Churches, and Denominations. In modern times, we have turned our backs on some of these prisons, only to build others. If we are not alert, the 'freedom' outlined in this book might well produce such a prison. For, as we shall see, modern man is able to seek the living God within himself at a much deeper level than was possible in previous generations; he can discover the infinity and eternity of God by examining those sciences which concern them-selves with the psychological working of men and the inter-woven beauty of the whole Universe. If we are not careful, therefore, we may simply return to a situation in which man himself once more becomes a prison for God.

This book makes no attempt to be complete. Many large subjects are not even mentioned, not least among them such testing matters as our changing systems of morality. Such subjects are considered by many people to be more important than those which follow; and they may well be right.

CHAPTER TWO

THE BIG GULF

The last Anglican Congress took place during the August of 1963. In the March of that year, John Robinson, Bishop of Woolwich, published his famous book *Honest to God*. Its effects were widely felt at the Congress meetings.

In spite of its vast sales, most Anglicans have not read it, and it received a mixed reception from the Church. The Archbishop of Canterbury, acting out what appeared to be a symbolic role, praised it in a pamphlet and then condemned it in a speech at Convocation. The rank and file of clergy and people, inside and outside the Church, ranged themselves in two well-defined groups, some praising and some blaming. Few remained neutral. At the Anglican Congress, when Bishop Robinson's book was referred to, there was great applause from some of the delegates while some sat firmly and dramatically on their hands.

To those who heard about the excited divisions among Church people before they actually read the book, the work itself must have come as a surprise and sometimes a disappointment. It is written in a style which is neither controversial nor lively. It is the work of a thoughtful and compassionate bishop, struggling with problems which have been nagging sensitive Christian minds for nearly a century. A large part of it consists of lengthy quotations from learned writers, not always modern ones.

Why then the fuss, amounting almost to hysteria? It would seem that the chief embarrassment arose from the fact that a clergyman of high rank, an established bishop of the Established Church of England and a gentleman, said honestly and openly what many people thought should have been kept under wraps. And, perhaps most upsetting, said it in English that the majority of readers could understand.

Monica Furlong, the well-known religious writer for the *Guardian*, expressed this admirably: 'Whatever positive good John Robinson's book had or had not achieved, it quickly became clear what its negative virtue was. It indicated just how deep and far-reaching was clerical contempt for the layman, how gravely the clergy under-rated his intelligence and understanding. The layman, as shoals of clerical letters unconsciously suggested, ought not to be allowed ideas which may upset or confuse him. Robinson's crime was to show uncompromisingly, that he believed he must "trust the people"; he could not be bothered with the tedious, over-scrupulous clerical language which never communicated. His problem does not appear to be doctrinal, but the problem of the sterility, the legalism, the lovelessness, which seem to choke and corrupt so many Christian pronouncements and actions.'

I think Miss Furlong is right. The gulf between clergy and laity is a wide one and it does not appear to be shrinking. I cannot offer evidence as massive as that shown in the response to Robinson's book, but such experience as I have had bears it out. When the Department of Religious Education first announced that it was indeed hoping that Pierre Berton would write a book to help church people understand an outsider's criticism of the institution, there was quick reaction. Many of the large number of letters received were highly critical of the decision. I am not concerned at the moment to suggest whether it was good or bad, but rather to mention a major reason offered by many writers to justify their position: that it would disturb the average layman.

When, in reply to a letter, I suggested in the W.A.'s *Living Message* that the Athanasian Creed might well be dropped from future revisions of the Prayer Book, I was not suggesting anything very unusual. The proposal has been made by many other people, some of them bishops. More important, it has already been acted upon by one of the larger Anglican Churches, the Protestant Episcopal Church in the United States of America, which has long since omitted it. In the replies I received, those which opposed my statement were all from clergy (two of them urging that I renounce my orders immediately); those which supported it all, with one exception, from layfolk.

David Frost, in a brilliant little *Punch* article called *Withoutness*, writes: 'In the pulpits up and down the land, clergymen are busy talking with that oddly special brand of distaste about "people who come home in the evening to their television sets and their washing machines and their record players." The congregation nods its head sadly in agreement. The clergyman may have a television set and a washing machine and record player, but oh, what a sign of Britain's moral decay that "people" should have their television sets and their washing machines and their record players.'

At a recent conference, a lay delegate, in the course of an enthusiastic address, said 'Clergy are like people.' The earnestness of his speech was swept away on a quickly-triggered wave of laughter. I am sure that innumerable conferences have produced examples of this type of slip and that the laughter is, in nearly all cases, immediate. It is all great fun, but it demonstrates how close to the surface is our awareness of the embarrassing chasm which exists between the priest and the layman.

Is this gulf a matter of pain to many or to few? There is no way of knowing, but it seems to me that here is one of those situations which calls for a very small, though uneasy, adjustment.

We have to cease thinking that there is some almighty difference between the priest and 'his' people. The old days, when the parson was the only educated man in the parish, or one of a small elite group, have gone. When he can offer advanced university training (and the proportion is rapidly declining) it will certainly be matched by large numbers of his congregation; and, even when this is not the case, the congregation is familiar with the modern world through television and newspapers. Parishioners no longer have to rely on the parson for their information; they no longer have to follow his lead when deciding what they ought to think or what the Christian attitude ought to be. The gulf between clergyman and layman was perhaps once a genuine one; it is now spurious. The parson is no longer 'the person' of the parish.

Nor is there a difference in spiritual quality, and any notion that there is such a difference was always a hoax. The idea that a clergyman somehow 'knows God' more closely than a layman flies in the face of the obvious facts. Whatever emotions are conjured up by the grand words used, the realities of life are the same for a clergyman as for a layman. They both have work to do which is part of God's world. Both of them are doing a job. The priest is as responsible for earning a living for his family as any member of the congregation. He is as susceptible to financial pressures as any trade union member, corporation executive, or casual laborer. The assumption made by his congregation is that he will move on to something better and that this will include a higher salary and higher status. They are generally, though not always, right in their assumption and there is no need to feel ashamed about it. The priest's duty to his wife and children is a primary one and he lives in a world where an increased salary means better education, better health, and better work. The complaint here is not that a clergyman operates by the same standards as a layman, but that the facts are too often shrouded in a fog of pious words which imply that money is not a strongly motivating force in the decisions clergy make.

I learned this lesson when I moved from my first curacy. In announcing the move, I explained to the congregation that I was being offered a wider and more challenging sphere of work (oh, those clerical words!), and that I felt impelled to make the move in spite of my deep desire to stay where I was. After the meeting was over, some appeared to take my statement at its face value. The majority, mostly the men, simply pumped my hand and congratulated me on a wise move. They also hoped that it would be the first of many. The implication was obvious. They saw me as a young executive and hoped that I would rise to the top in a business corporation which happens to be known as the Church. I remember most vividly, however, a lady who offered me a pair of delicately arched gloved fingers and, with the satirical twinkle which only middle-aged spinsters can achieve, said: 'You must feel very *proud*.'

Let us chop down the verbiage and move into real life. The parson is primarily a human being, and the nearer he draws to the so-called laymen who surround him, the more he 'fulfils his Vocation'.

Occasionally the idea circulates that a clergyman's training is a deep and great preparation for the spiritual life and that this enables him to live at a level higher than that on which his congregation lives. It is, therefore, necessary to insist that the training received by a man preparing for the ministry is a guarantee of nothing. My own seminary was as near useless as it is possible to imagine, most of the training being an exercise in medieval logic chopping of the most comical variety. To use Miss Furlong's words, we were thoroughly prepared to read, write, and think in a dead, legalistic and loveless manner.

Instead of being helped to come to an understanding of God and his ways with man, we were offered massive proofs of God's existence (which turned out to be no proofs at all), long lists of God's attributes (which had no bearing on anything), and a history of Theism (which involved high sounding words of Latin length but no noticeable meaning). The examinations we took in order to 'qualify' for ordination were as remote from parish or national life as Caesar's Gallic War.

I mention this fairly ancient matter for two reasons. In the first place, my generation provides the present-day Church with many of its ministers, and it would be grossly misleading to let laymen think that our training helped us to any spiritual superiority. In the second place, although many theological seminaries have improved considerably and many of them are surging ahead into the twentieth century, the fact remains that a large number still supply the ordin- and with the same dreary lecture-type information that was delivered to my own generation twenty-five years ago. And this information often bears little or no relationship to the complex problems of the modern world.

The Rev. Charles Feilding has recently conducted an extensive survey of the work done in Canadian and American seminaries. His report, shortly to be made available, states that there has been very little change either in method or content of teaching during the past twenty-five years. In addition to his severe criticism of the situation in theological colleges and seminaries, he is also planning a pilot project which will examine the possibilities of field training for the preparation of a 'professional Christian ministry'.

Readers of this book can probably do little about the college situation, though perhaps one or two may raise their voices to urge a radical change in the type of training offered. They can, however, ask themselves whether the time is ripe for a Church in which there is no distinction of quality between clergyman and layman, in which we have a common ministry.

Such common ministries are becoming numerous and, whenever they are accepted, there comes a sense of freedom, which leads quickly to deeper spiritual awareness.

This is felt strongly by clergy. Many a parson, finding that his life is no different from that of his parishioners, has often in the past become aware of a sense of guilt. It is as though, having said, 'I am just like my parishioners', he goes on to add, 'I should be different'.

But why? The highest honor that can be conferred on any creature is to be a human being, and the search for ourselves is one that can never end. At a conference held recently, a rector in a study group declared, 'I wish I could just go down to the curling rink and be a human being like my congregation.' He had made a supreme discovery, which freed him from a load of guilt as surely as the bundle rolled off Christian's back in *Pilgrim's Progress*. It was a burden he should never have been forced to bear. Whatever gifts are needed in order to minister to people, being better than they are is not one of them.

The discovery of a common ministry can also be a liberating one for any layman who makes it. Many are at the moment weighed down with the completely unnecessary load of guilt which destroys the priest. It is as though, even when they do not express it, they sense a great gap between what they actually believe and what they think they *ought* to believe. Somehow, they feel, they should have more Faith, so that they could believe the great things that the clergy appear to believe so strongly.

An Anglican priest recently attended a synagogue service with a friend who deeply admired the rabbi who was conducting the ceremony. As the rabbi read solemnly from the Law, the friend sighed and, leaning over to his companion, whispered in an awed voice: 'You see that man. He actually knows what it means.' Many an Anglican worshipper has the same feeling, if only in residual form. There, in the pulpits and before the altars (he thinks) stand the men who know clearly the Faith which their lips proclaim. They are the men who are unworldly, who have denied the self, who know God, who hear him speak, who are called in a dramatic way to their vocation, who pray real prayers, whose thoughts do not wander, and for whom the Catechism is a simple statement of facts.

As we have already discovered, there is little substance to this and, with the publication of *Honest to God*, laymen were suddenly faced with the freedom-giving realization that we are all much the same. For John Robinson, a bishop who had gone through everything clerical and even been born into it, had come out and said that he shared the problems of the layman, that he too found difficulty in believing certain dogmas. Moreover, he said that there was no need to believe them and that much of what appeared to be junk was, in fact, junk.

Two years later, the bishop is still a bishop, still writing, and still being discussed and debated. But more than that has happened. Bishop Pike is more widely read than ever, and sharpening many of Robinson's ideas. More clergy are becoming outspoken about their doubts and fears, and learning that Faith is deepened rather than destroyed as unnecessary barnacles (very pretty barnacles, sometimes) are scraped off. And more laymen, in spite of misgivings and a realization of what responsibility lies ahead of them, are seeing the truth through the clouds of centuries. A leading layman recently stated, 'Either the clergy give up controlling everything, or the Church collapses.' I think he is right.

The adjustment called for is not a great one, but it requires courage. To walk into freedom is not easy because there is always the fear of what may happen. The clergyman may be afraid to lose his status (largely imaginary, nowadays) and his authority. Give laymen their head, he thinks, and where will it all lead? From the grimy caves of history, the ugly dragon of Heresy begins to roar. Yet the fear, like most fears, is self-created and, as Saint John points out realistically, is cast out by love. If Jesus' words are only a fraction of the truth, we cannot possibly become mature Christians unless we surrender the little crumbs of authority to which we cling so tenaciously. Freedom means that we have to move into the market-square and take our chances with anyone else. We can no longer be carried by the rest of society;* when we speak foolishness, we cannot complain if it is printed in the newspapers or protested by other clergy and people. It is a freedom which comes directly from Christ, who claimed no privileges for himself, who took his chances, and who never stood upon his dignity.

For the layman, the change called for by the new movements of the Church can produce similar fears. In particular, it means that he is now responsible before God and the people. So long as the priest is thought of as a person on a pedestal, he can be expected

---

*I am thinking here of the way clergy are sometimes given preferential treatment, allowed to jump lines of people waiting for some service, admitted into the doctor's or lawyer's office by some special arrangement, given ten per cent off in stores, given preferential income tax arrangements, protected from unemployment, invited to head tables. At a deeper level I am thinking of the cruelties practised against clergy who do not toe the line of their superior's moral principles, of the closed doors presented to men who have been dubbed failures—and all without the sort of public criticism which would befall any government leader who did the same thing.

to pronounce on all difficult questions. And, greatest of all luxuries, there is no need to agree with him. So there comes into being the parish which insists that the priest make all the decisions and yet which criticizes him constantly. Such a congregation has no sense of responsibility. All is the priest's work. If things go well, then he is applauded; if they go badly, he is blamed.

The freedom that comes with realizing that there is no pedestal and no difference means that the layman can no longer hide under the rector's cassock. The state of the church becomes the state of the laymen, and their health is its health.

Therefore, he finds himself not only freed, but freed to act. He no longer expects the clergyman to hold his hand. He expects that, as partners, they will move into the complex areas of modern life. Realizing that there is no good work without constant re-training in the modern world, he will expect his priest to be away from the parish every five years (more or less) to take a three months program. And he will expect to pay for this. In other words, sitting in a pew will mean that he feels himself a vital member of the Church and not a customer to be pampered. If he needs counselling, he will go to his priest, which may mean that the priest will refer him to a professional worker in the relevant field. Otherwise, he will expect no more of his rector than that he become a man.

You may feel that this modern approach will lead one day to a Church which does not need clergy. If you do, then I suggest you examine the thought carefully and without fear.

CHAPTER THREE

A PRISON FOR GOD

'I should see the garden far better,' said Alice to herself, 'if I could get to the top of that hill. And here's a path that leads straight to it—' Unfortunately, every time she tried to follow the path to the top of the hill, she found herself walking into the house where her adventures had begun.

She did not give up. 'Resolutely turning her back on the house, she set out once more down the path, determined to keep straight on till she got to the hill. For a few minutes all went well, and she was just saying, "I really *shall* do it this time—", when the path gave a sudden twist and shook itself (as she described it afterward), and the next moment she found herself actually walking in at the door.

' "Oh, it's too bad!" she cried. "I never saw such a house for getting in the way! Never!" '

We could have a good deal of amusement playing the above incident in a variety of ways. If God were thought of as the hill, for example, what is the house which keeps getting in the way?

I don't wish to use Alice's adventure, however, as an analogy, but simply to remind ourselves that we sometimes come closer to our objective when we walk away from it than when we chase it ardently.

I think that this principle set out by Carroll—who was, you may remember, a clergyman—applies very much to how we think of God. For centuries, we have tried desperately to come nearer to understanding him, but as we have done so, have constantly found ourselves further away. In my last chapter, I mentioned the 'attributes' of God which we learned at my theological seminary. As a curate, I was under the delusion that by grabbing at God in this way, we could really come closer to understanding him. I therefore preached a series of Lenten sermons on the subject. As the congregation moved further and further into polite inattention, I became

13

more anxious. 'I really *shall* get through next time,' I thought. After several weeks of desperate struggling against the unwilling listeners, I finally said to the Vicar: 'To hell with it all. They just don't want to know God.' 'Try not bothering,' he suggested. It was the best advice he ever gave me.

My error was obvious. I had been trying to bring God into a position where I could pin him down and feel that he had become my property; and this has been the trap into which man's anxiety has led him throughout history. It has not, moreover, been limited to those religions which our snobbery used to describe as 'pagan', and which tried to box God up in a tree or a totem pole. One of the most ancient and sacred symbols known to the early Hebrew nation was the 'Ark', called amongst other things 'the Ark of the Covenant'. It was probably an oblong chest of acacia or shittim wood; in it God was thought to dwell personally and to guide the march of his people into the holy land. Its later history is complicated and eventually it passes out of existence. At all times, people believed that it pinned God down to such an extent that they could feel safe in its presence. When, therefore, the Philistines stole it, it was as though they had stolen God.

Not all prisons come in wood or stone. The most impregnable are constructed of words, and it is of words that the most successful prisons for God have been fashioned. A classic example is the Law, which caused Saint Paul so much difficulty. Originally the many injunctions which Moses gave were clearly intended to free the people from the apathy which beset them in the middle of their long and fearful journey through the desert. The very success of the Law proves how appropriate it was. Given, as Jesus points out, 'for the sinfulness of your hearts', it helped the tribes establish satisfactory standards for their life.

The Law was an expression of God's love for his people—not the only expression, but the response which he made at a certain difficult time in their history. Unfortunately, for perhaps the highest motives, the religious leaders of the nation saw a chance to box God up. Here, they declared, we have at last identified the living God. He may constantly elude us with his 'I am that I am', and we may not know his name, but we can see him clearly in his Law.

When Jesus lived his life, we see the end result of a sad process. The scribes and pharisees honestly thought that God was to be seen and obeyed in the washing of pots, fasting, observing sabbaths and new moons, stoning adulterous women and so on. Nor does Jesus say that the Law was stupid or that it had no validity. He simply declares that it must not act as a prison for God. Jehovah (he says) once declared to his people: 'Thou shalt love thy neighbour and hate thine enemy'. It was a declaration to them at a certain time in their history and likely the most they were able to hear. But God was not speaking for all time. His law is a free one, which means that it changes and develops. '*I* say unto you,' asserts Jesus, 'that you shall love your enemies.'

At Pentecost, Saint Peter, taking up the liberating words of the prophet Joel, stated categorically that the Spirit of God was now poured upon all flesh, that God now revealed himself through *everyone*. The old restrictions, which limited the interpretation of his word to a select number of important religious leaders, were now gone. Jesus had freed men from their sin and also from the shackles of the Law.

But the shackles were soon to return. In the name of Jesus himself, a professional elite set themselves up as the men through whose mouths God spoke and, having convinced the people of this, proceeded once more to tie God up and imprison him in new arks made of new words. As with the old arks and the old laws, there was much good, and many of the declarations which these early Christian leaders made are as valid today as they ever were. But they are not the whole expression of God and, if they are treated as prisons for him and for his people, they are wrongly used.

Take, for example, the Creeds. Originally they served a magnificent purpose and the truths they declared were important. No matter how unhappy we may be about the tyrannical way in which they were imposed, the fact remains that they were accepted and acceptable. Like the original Law of Moses, they spoke to a real need in Christian congregations.

As time has passed, the ways in which we can accept these Creeds have changed. The Athanasian Creed has fared the worst. Originally designed for a specific and necessary purpose—the answering of a powerful and popular heresy—its language and mode of thought have become more and more remote for more and more people. The Nicene Creed, containing some straightforward statements as well as some abstruse philosophising, has proved lustier. Unfortunately, many of its clauses deal with problems which no longer concern the average person, and it is no surprise to learn from Bishop Pike that it was nearly excluded from the American Prayer Book.

The Apostles' Creed sounds a more convincing note. If, as is generally supposed, it was pieced together in some way to prepare candidates for baptism, we can see that it would try to express the central teachings of the Faith and not to answer some heresy of the day. It is, therefore, as magnificent a hymn to our beliefs as it was when it was first used. But is it more? In the past, most Christians would have replied 'Yes'—that it is a statement of specific beliefs by which we test our Faith; and that, if we do not accept them, then doubt may be cast on our right to be considered churchmen. Many people still think in this way; but many others do not. At all events, there is one conclusion which seems inevitable. It should never be used as a prison in which to imprison God. Yet this is sometimes tried. In the Spring of 1964, a questionnaire was circulated, to which 248 clergy (out of 400) replied. One of the questions was: Do you believe in the literal truth of the Apostles' Creed? In reply, 154 said 'Yes—fully'; 63 said 'With most of it'; 6 said 'With part only'; 9 said 'No'; and 15 gave no answer. The first reply, however, needs to be broken down a little because some, who noted 'Yes—fully', also suggested that they could not take such phrases as 'ascended' literally.

At some later date, it is hoped to pursue this question more deeply. For the moment, it is obvious that the Apostles' Creed nowadays poses problems to the believer which are comparatively new, and that it is becoming increasingly difficult to regard it as a formula which expresses in rigid and final form the mind of God.

The fact is that all attempts to imprison God are doomed at their start and, as men's minds are open to his guidance, they find that previous formulae no longer prove adequate. They are not saying that the formulae were wrong or misguided but that, in their literal form, they have become a matter of history. God works with us in the present and guides us in the present. The Apostles' Creed (to use our example) is in the present, to be used and interpreted in the thought forms of today, and not those of yesterday.

CHAPTER FOUR

WHAT IS GOD LIKE? – PART I

Once we realize that God cannot be boxed up in a tabernacle, a Creed, or even Church and Sacraments, we are freed to look back through history and see how often and how radically those who believed in him have changed their ideas of what he is like. This constant change is not a modern event; it goes back to the beginning of man's search for God and can be seen vividly illustrated in the pages of the Bible.

Many Christians, reading the Old Testament, find in themselves a certain embarrassment which springs from the marked difference of approach between the early writers and those of today's Church. Faced with this uneasiness, they detect in themselves a pressure to neglect the Old Testament and to concentrate their attention on the New; and, in doing this, they fall into an old trap.

In the early Church, a man called Marcion, suffering the same embarrassment, suggested that the Old Testament should be dropped from the Christian Bible. He was condemned as a heretic and there can be no question that to have accepted his proposal would have been a tragedy. We need the Old Testament, partly because without it the Gospel would be mutilated and partly because it stands in its own right as a running commentary on God's dealings with man and man's with God.

And yet, as with most heresies, Marcion's attitude survives in practice more widely than is supposed. There are, it is true, certain parts of the Old Testament where the Christian feels at home, but there are others where he finds himself bewildered. These last passages are a closed book to us and, when read in Church, are received with closed ears. The intricate food laws of Leviticus, the prescribed punishments for a wide variety of offences, the assumption that a man might rightly have many wives and concubines, the status given to women generally, the acceptance of slavery, to name but a few, are either unknown to the average Christian, or like the *Song of Solomon*, explained or edited away.

The embarrassment reaches its peak when we examine the portraits of God which are offered in the Old Testament. For they seem to be different from those which we are nowadays developing and which we see in Christ. It is as though there are two voices speaking to us, and both of them with authority. The first says: 'I cannot believe that God could approve the killing of innocent children so long as it is for his glory. I cannot see the glory and I cannot believe that he would desire it this way.' The other says: 'It's the Bible I'm reading. Surely the Bible must be right. If I say I don't believe one part of it, I may be saying I don't believe any of it. I may be saying I don't believe in God.'

Yet, if what has been said so far is correct, the problem vanishes. A portrait of God is not God himself. If we say that we cannot accept the idea that God loves the massacre of children, we are saying that we cannot accept the particular ideas of the narrator when he wrote them this way. We believe that God is a God of Love. We have no reason to suppose that the writer believed otherwise; but we may feel that some of the consequences seem to have escaped him.

We are, therefore, able to read the Old Testament portraits of God with a new freedom. For if God, in the Bible which is his Word, permits men to change, to discover new concepts, to tread a path which leads them from something old to something new; and if, as the Bible itself makes clear, the new is often better than the old; then the same will be true of the twentieth century. God continues his work. We make new discoveries about him and they are not the same as the old. If the process of change was blessed by God in the second century before Christ, during Christ's own life, during the first five centuries of the Christian era, during the Middle Ages and at the Reformation—then we need not worry. It is not stretching Faith too far to say that he blesses the same process today.

It may even be that we are now ready to prepare a Third Testament, which will not replace the former ones, but fulfil them. Just as it proved absurd to believe that God's revelation of himself ceased with the Pentateuch and the Prophets, so it is absurd to think that it ceased with the New Testament. A modern Testament would admittedly be long in preparing. Sheer quantity would prove a problem, as would the principles of selection. It might, in fact, take several hundreds of years. But, when done, it would have upon it a different face from what had gone before. It would include much from many different sources, not all of them theological. Theology, in fact, might well provide only a small segment.

Nor, indeed, would it be limited to the written word. Methods of communication have multiplied, and we have only begun to nibble at the edges of what will happen when we finally grasp their significance. A Third Testament might, in fact, prove inadequate; the next few centuries could well produce several.

At the moment, however, we are concerned with the changing ideas of God which occur in the Bible as we now have it. The following brief description follows a roughly chronological path; but two warnings need to be made. First, it is not implied that later ideas are *necessarily* better than earlier ones. There are many lapses and the movement is not always forward. Second, it is not implied that later ideas displaced earlier ones. Life is much too complicated for such a facile assumption. The later ideas of the prophets are to be found in many of the words of the patriarchs. Nor is any change completely accepted, even by those who put it forward. Thus the so-called 'God of Wrath' is not displaced, but continues into the prophets, the New Testament, and through to the present.

Here, then, are a few key events in the history of the Church when there was a clear and radical change made in the answer to the question: what is God like?

In the earliest writings of the Old Testament, God is portrayed very much as if he were human. He walks about the Garden of Eden in the cool of the day and acts, to our modern eyes, very much like a pampered, though powerful, child. With the great era of the patriarchs, we are introduced to a description of God which resembles that of a benevolent, oriental tyrant; a jealous God, who is apt to be angry (often for what appear to be trivial reasons), quite unpredictable, susceptible to flattery, kindly to those who obey him implicitly, and anxious for the welfare of his chosen people.

As the nation becomes more powerful, so God resembles more a warrior king. The fact comes to us with stark and unmistakeable clarity. He is happy that innocent women and children should be massacred, so long as it is in his name. Looking back, we can see what happened. God is, we believe, the God of compassion and so he always was. But he granted man free will and the religious leaders of these early days found their ears waxed tight by their own prejudices and anxieties. They were, above all, determined that Jehovah should be triumphant over his enemies; and so they heard him say, 'Go kill, for so shall my kingdom be established.' He urged his people to slay their enemies and spare none. To him the psalmist responded: 'Break the teeth of the ungodly, O God, in their mouths; . . . the righteous shall rejoice when he seeth the vengeance: he shall wash his footsteps in the blood of the ungodly, so that a man shall say, Verily there is a reward for the righteous: verily he is a God who judgeth the earth'; 'God shall wound the head of thine enemies, and the tongue of thy dogs may be red through the same. It is seen, O God, how thou goest'; and 'Let their eyes be blinded, that they see not'.*

I have selected a few of many illustrations from the Psalms because they occur in a book which is familiar to Christians and which we use constantly in our worship. Is it possible to agree with the wishes of the psalmist? Could we honestly ask that the modern atheist's days be few, his children fatherless, his wife a widow, his children vagabonds and that 'there be no man to pity him, nor to have compassion upon his fatherless children'? Could we honestly say to the modern persecutor of the Church, 'blessed shall he be that taketh thy children and throweth them against the stones'?

I am assuming that the answer will, in each case, be an unequivocal 'no'. The portrait of God implied in these passages is a portrait which we cannot accept. There is no judgement to be made here. We do not know what provoked the psalmist's bitterness. I can imagine a victim of Hitler's concentration camps crying the same words as his ancestors did beside the waters of Babylon; and I could not find it possible to say anything more than, 'I understand'. No judgement, then, can be made of the old writers. But, if we were to pretend that their portraits are literally valid for us in the comforts of modern Canada, then we would be under judgement, and deserve to be. It is good to note that the revisers of the latest Canadian Prayer Book have at last suppressed these verses, which can clearly form no part

*It is almost impossible to decide when many of the Psalms were written and some of these quotations may, in fact, spring from a later period.

of our worship, though we may well read them to discover how close to the surface lies the bitterness of mankind.*

With the Prophets came a radical change in the idea of God, perhaps the biggest change until the present day. As with all such changes, they met with the same types of response. Some people saw what the prophets were trying to say, and tried to understand it. Some turned a deaf ear, preferring to listen to other, smoother talkers, who prophesied the old ways and urged no change. Still others, deeply immersed in the past glories of Israel and the Lord Jehovah Almighty, found the whole approach of the Prophets distasteful and even blasphemous. This last group may even have been in a majority because Jesus says to his disciples: 'Blessed are ye when men shall revile you and persecute you. Rejoice, for so persecuted they the prophets which were before you.'

Yet it is the radical idea which survives in the records,† summed up in Micah's perceptive words: 'He hath showed thee, O man, what is good; and what doth the Lord require of thee, but to do justly, and to love mercy, and to walk humbly with thy God.'‡ This is not completely new, of course, but it seemed revolutionary to his contemporaries. Perhaps, however, the most startling portrait is offered by Hosea. The God he portrays is, above all, compassionate beyond any normal human practice. He is likened to a husband who pursues an unfaithful woman time after time. There is no limit to the number of occasions on which he will take her back. How far this is from the oriental tyrant who revenged himself on his enemies! 'Love a woman beloved of her friend and an adulteress, even as the Lord loveth the children of Israel,' says the God of Hosea.

The God of the great days of Old Testament history not only delighted in power but in rituals and sacrifices. He could, it was thought, be satisfied when altars were built to a certain size, prayers

---

*See *The Lord of the Flies* by William Golding, a novel which brings this home very vividly.

†Mixed with other ideas, of course. All the prophets did not, at all times, in everything they said, realize the full extent of what they were declaring. In the middle of the essential portrait of God which they offered, we can still find trace of a God who supported punishment and war.

‡Several rabbis have told me that this is perhaps one of the most typical Jewish texts today. Also, that the old bloodthirsty injunctions are now being re-interpreted.

offered in certain ways, sacrifices made under certain conditions, precise tasks performed on certain days, and rest taken on others.

There were good reasons for this and, when trying to assess the skill with which the chosen race occupied the promised land and established their God-centred society in a hostile world, we can see how necessary it was that the things of Jehovah should be carefully ordered and settled. When the Prophets came to interpret God's word, however, they saw that there had been a change. They did not deny the value of strict rituals and ceremonial, but they realized that the type of offering demanded in the days of Moses was not a pattern for all time or for all places. Through their lips, we see a different portrait of God taking shape, a God to whom altars, sacrifices, feast days and fast days are acceptable but no longer essential. Sincerity and a sense of purpose are the basic demands, and so the God of Isaiah cries: 'Incense is an abomination unto me. The new moon and sabbaths, the calling of assemblies, I cannot away with; it is iniquity, even the solemn meeting. Your new moons and your feasts my soul hateth; they are a trouble unto me; I am weary to bear them. And when ye spread forth your hands, I will hide mine eyes from you; yea, when ye make many prayers, I will not hear.' The God of Amos echoes these words: 'I hate, I despise your feast days, and I will not smell in your solemn assemblies. Take away from me the noise of thy songs.'

The quotations could go on endlessly. The God presented to us by Isaiah, Hosea and Amos is the same God whom Abraham, Moses, and Jacob worshipped, but the portrait is vastly different. This does not mean that the later descriptions have nothing in common with the earlier: it does mean that God reveals himself constantly and that each generation has to interpret that revelation. To this task we are called just as much as the generations whose response is reported in the Bible.

CHAPTER FIVE

WHAT IS GOD LIKE? – PART II

For Christians, God is fully revealed in Jesus Christ. Once more we are faced with a familiar problem. The most direct relationship between God and Man comes in the personal life of an individual. But each man is set in a community of other men and cannot make any valid decisions without the aid of that community. So the Christ has to be interpreted by one man to another, and we are faced with many interpretations and interpreters. Christ comes to us seen through the eyes of different writers, translators, artists, musicians, and takes final shape when we make our own reading of the events. The portrait of Christ in Saint Mark is different from that in Saint John; that presented by Patterson Smythe is not the same as that presented by Philip Carrington; that which exists in your mind is not the same as that which exists in mine.

Yet, in spite of the inevitable difficulties of communication, the portrait of God in the biblical accounts of Jesus is sharper even than that of the prophets.

Moreover, if we believe that in Jesus we are encountering God directly, then we may with value notice how many are the revolutionary changes he made in the religion and beliefs of his day. For him the Faith was never static. He imprisoned nobody in the Law or even the Prophets; he offered and followed no Creeds (though he did not condemn them unless they acted as prisons); and the Spirit which breathed through him was the free Spirit of God, which blows where he wishes and is not bound by past events. Very few people understood Jesus, and it is no surprise that the leaders of Church and State, who valued discipline above freedom, opposed him.

We can only look at a few points here, but they are significant.
1. Jesus was tried for blasphemy.* From the point of view of the

---

*This was the declared reason. The real reasons probably lay elsewhere.

authorities and the strict interpretation of the Faith (the Law), it was a true charge. The Prophets were not used as evidence because the Prophets had always seemed blasphemous and always will do, as we can see from the way Bishops Robinson and Pike are received by many today.

2. Jesus made it clear that God was only interested in the 'heart of man' and was therefore not influenced by rituals, ceremonials, sabbaths and new moons, eye-catching forms of prayer, openly practised fasting, priests and other religious leaders. The test seems to have been that all these were made for man and not man for them.

3. He made it clear that God is above all concerned about man. He taught very little of what we call doctrine, and was constantly confusing his religious listeners by allowing the state of the person he was helping to control what he said and did. This was confusing because it had often been assumed that we should start with God's declared Law and then make people fit it. Now there came a man who seemed to be reversing the process. We can understand their difficulties, because Jesus' approach has rarely been followed in the Church or even outside it. Towards the end of the nineteenth century, the old fashioned atheist writers of the Rationalist Press Association had a field day taking different passages from Jesus' words and showing that they 'contradicted' each other. They missed the whole point and assumed, as too many Christians do, that Jesus' words were a sort of new Law. As soon as we see that Jesus was not bound in any way by legal principles or precedents, but was interested solely in the people he was helping, then we are freed from any need to turn his words into a self-consistent body of principles.

4. Jesus was interested in neither race nor religion, except as the servants of man. He was prepared to support people, like the Samaritans, who were despised by orthodox churchmen as immoral atheists. He did not say that they were necessarily closer to God, but that the religious convictions of the Priest and Levite were insignificant when set against the kindly action of the Samaritan who helped a wounded traveller or the Samaritan leper who remembered to say thank you.

5. Jesus made it clear that God was not concerned about the literal carrying out of the Law, though there was no merit, either, in

breaking it. For Him, the Law was there, neither good nor bad in itself. Made for man, it was good if it helped him, bad if it imprisoned him. It was perhaps this attitude, as much as any, which led to the charge of blasphemy. As Saint Paul was to remark later: 'God hath made us ministers of the new testament; not of the letter, but of the spirit; for the letter killeth, but the spirit giveth life.'—a text which should be engraved on the walls of every magistrates' court.

I remember when I first read the New Testament. It came as a shock to realize that the God portrayed there was the God of the past two thousand years, for the God who came to me through the lips of the leaders of Church and State in England was jealous, possessive and punishing. When the insurance companies wished to indicate some meaningless tragedy they called it an Act of God. Whenever some cruel event took the life or health of a poor child or adult, the people around nodded their heads and said, 'It's God's will.' When a great friend of mine lay in agony, he confided, 'I could die in peace. If only they'd stop telling me God loves me.'

The judges of the land sent men to long terms of imprisonment and even death under the delusion that they were somehow doing the right thing by God. When, occasionally, a voice was raised in protest against the barbarism of capital punishment, a large proportion of the newspaper letters which urged its retention came from religious people speaking in the name of God.

What had happened? It is difficult to say, and the historians must provide the answer. It may be that the Emperor Constantine, who became a Christian and spread 'the Faith' by force, tempted Church leaders to think in terms of power and ambition in order to achieve an arbitrary rule over a now subservient population. At all events, the Church *did* achieve power and this power became vested in the hands of the higher clergy. The process reached its climax in the Middle Ages, when the unholy alliance known as the Holy Roman Empire set the pattern for Christian method.

There were great and wonderful exceptions, of course, and prophets such as Huss and Wycliffe, More and Latimer, paid the same price as their forebears. For the God of the One, Holy, Catholic, and Apostolic Church was presented by the great powers as a God who tolerated death by torture, massacre, persecution, and war so long as it was conducted in his name. The men who fought the Crusades were not hypocritical. They simply saw God as wanting the Turks to be destroyed. The modern Christian who supports nuclear warfare, capital punishment and prisons which punish without mercy, is not hypocritical. He simply sees God as a punishing God.

The medieval pattern changed surprisingly little after the Reformation, and the angry God of the feudal system was accepted by most of the new denominations. Examples of this are innumerable, and it would not be exaggerating to say that nearly all attempts made over the past four centuries to improve the condition of the poor and weak have been opposed by the great ones of the Church as well as the State. Fantastic as it may seem to us, denunciations of what we now see clearly to have been God's acts, were made in the name of God himself. Attempts to abolish the death penalty for sheep stealing, to ease the pains of childbirth, to aid family planning, to support the unemployed, to destroy prison walls, to introduce anaesthetics, to give the worker rights and financial rewards equal to those of his employer, to abolish capital punishment, to ensure universal free education and universal free medical care—all these, and many more, have been opposed by Christian people and often in the name of the Lord.

As I have already pointed out, there is no cause to point any fingers here. The people who opposed reforms in God's name were not hypocritical. Like the Crusaders before them, they simply expressed belief in a God who approved of punishment as a noble weapon in the hands of the righteous.

And yet we may feel a need to protest that it is a strange God who is willing to approve, or even tolerate, suffering. Certainly a strange God to set alongside the Christ who fought suffering and who condemned rigid self-righteous rules as much as he attacked high-sounding moralities.

Throughout this period, of course, many Christian voices were raised in loud protest against such a portrait of God. Coming from all Churches and sects, their message was shot through with the concept declared by the Prophets and perfected in Christ—namely, that God is Love, and that no amount of rationalization can square this with heavy punishments, suffering, imprisonments, inequalities, or lack of brotherhood.

CHAPTER SIX

THE GOD OF TODAY'S WORLD

And so we come to the present. It is difficult to interpret one's own day, but I think the big challenge offered to us now is being given and answered by a growing number of men and women in the Church, including such great writers as Bonhoeffer, Tillich, Williams, Berger, Robinson, Pike, Stringfellow, Furlong, Pelz, Warren and many more.

What are these writers saying? In general terms, they are challenging us to throw away the chains with which we have for centuries been trying to bind God. The portrait of God which is offered to us in all these writers is one who has never ceased to create, who is constantly changing and modifying his creation and, above all, the human beings who seem to lie at its heart.

It is an exciting idea this, that God is everywhere, that we meet him wherever we are, and that his creation is very good. One wonders how it came to be suppressed for so long by so many worthy people. It was expressed in crystal fashion by Dr. Warren's speech at the Anglican Congress which has turned out to be a Theme Address for the whole Church.

Its keynote was sounded in these words: 'God meets me everywhere, or I never meet him. If I think I meet him only in Bible and Sacrament, and in the Christian fellowship, then I do not know who it is I meet. For he speaks to me in my newspaper as well as in the Bible. He seeks me out in the theatre, in the novel, in art as well as in the Holy Communion.' He might have added, 'in the laboratory and on the race track, in the tavern and the flop house.'

This is a fantastic thought, even though simply expressed. If we ever believed that God was in any way tied to our tabernacles and churches, our parishes and synods, our clergy and servers, we can forget it now. He has escaped into the whole world, where he was all the time.

So it is that, when we wish to seek a portrait of God, we seek it not only in the Bible and Church History but in Sociology, Psychology, Science, Poetry, Music (the Beatles as well as Beethoven), and so on to the end of the list of human activities.

For we are rapidly realizing that, if the Incarnation means anything, it means that man matters, and matters beyond measure. The highest calling I have is to be a man, and Jesus considered it so for himself. The old phrase, 'made in the image of God' has, in the twentieth century, taken on a whole new range of meaning. For we are finding out much more about man, more of his infinity, more of his timelessness, more of his depth, more of his endless variety. 'What a piece of work is a man!' declared Hamlet, and we can now supply more than enough evidence to justify his words.*

In his theme address, Max Warren said: 'Think of that Viennese psychoanalyst who, studying the diseased minds of innumerable patients, first charted the unknown continent of man's unconscious. . . . (and we) will humbly thank God for his grace at work in Sigmund Freud, no less at work because Freud did not acknowledge him.'

And one of the most significant discoveries which has followed from the work of Freud and other pioneers is that people can rarely be dismissed with such labels as 'wicked' or 'damned'. Whether we like it or not, we are all bound up intimately with our heredity and environment. The way in which we live can only be interpreted completely by God. When men attempt to interpret, they can only go a short way. In the mid-twentieth century, we can however go far enough to see that standards of behavior are essentially relative and can perceive why it was that Jesus became so angry about people who judged others.

The realization that a man's behavior is beyond complete human analysis follows upon many changes in the whole attitude of men towards each other. It was once thought that a lunatic was a sinful man, and that his madness ought to be beaten out of him. To punish him, even to the cruellest extremes, was not thought of as being ungodly. Rather, it was considered to be one way of carrying out God's clear will: was not his voice declared against the insane per-

---

*It is also part of Hamlet's fretful tragedy that he has to add: 'And yet, to me, what is this quintessence of dust? Man delights not me, nor woman neither.'

son? Everyone now can see that the madman is a full human being, just like ourselves, who needs help, compassion and healing. It seems strange to us that any Christian could beat a madman and not appreciate how far his conduct was removed from that of the Messiah he (very sincerely) worshipped.

But there is no point in looking at the errors of the past unless it keeps us from repeating them. And we are repeating them. For what has been said of the madman may be said now (often, if not always) of the homosexual, the prostitute, the hysteric, the thief, the murderer, the liar, and so on. Whenever we find ourselves saying, 'the only thing such and such a criminal can understand is the cat of nine tails' or 'keep him locked up, that's what I say,' or 'capital punishment must be retained,' let us remember the men who flogged the insane person and felt that it was right to do so.

Some of these discoveries about human nature lie a long way in the past, but they are now being dramatized and felt by more and more people. It is no longer unusual to say that a criminal is a sick man and that to put him in prison is no use at all, let alone charitable. Remembering Jesus's insistence that we judge not lest we be judged, and re-inforcing it with the parables of the servant who refused to forgive and that of the sheep and the goats, we are now at last realizing that it is not possible for one human being to judge another in any context.

This is not to say that courts and sentences ought to end, for there will always be need to protect the sick person from himself. What is being said is this: that we treat the criminal or the pervert in the same way as we treat any other sick person. This means that we must try to heal him while, at the same time, we protect society. Faced with a victim of diptheria, we do not let him roam free. We look after him. Hospitals and rest homes deprive him of his freedom, but he is not denigrated or treated as if he owed a debt to society. Faced with an insane person, we do not leave him to his own devices: we treat him with the same care and respect for his dignity as we treat the Prime Minister. The modern plea is that we treat the murderer and the thief as the sick men they are.

What is God like in our modern portrait? A grandmother? Scarcely. He is the God of Love above anything else. We can separate ourselves from him and so become the victims of what has traditionally been called Sin. But this separation is a difficult thing to assess and no human being has a right to do so. We are at last beginning to take Jesus' statements seriously. The religious leaders of his day took the view that sins could be detected by their outward signs. Many of our own religious leaders take the same view. But they are all warned by Christ that this is not possible. How often Jesus seemed to turn topsy-turvy the accepted moral standards of his day, by showing that the simple-minded tax-gatherer was more justified than the church-going, tithing, praying Pharisee; that the unbelieving and immoral Samaritan came closer to God than the clergyman or lawyer of the Established Church and State; that the dishonest steward was to be praised; that the sabbath should be broken if it hindered men; and so on.

We can easily translate this into modern terms. The man sent to jail for drunken behavior may be closer to God than the self-righteous magistrate who sends him there; the priest who is denied his right to minister in a parish may be closer than the bishop who penalizes him; the homo-sexual may be nearer to God than the hetero-sexual person who denounces him.

Our understanding today of human relationships (and we have not even mentioned the infinite variety of human personality raised by modern analysis), has helped us to see a relationship between God and Man and so have in our minds a picture of God. It is one of reconciliation, forgiveness, charity, and acceptance. It has taken us nearly two thousand years to take Christ seriously, but we have at last reached the point of beginning.

The change we are called upon to make today is one by which we realize that the portrait of God as a tyrant with exclusive interest in a few clearly-identified people, has been set aside. God is free.

CHAPTER SEVEN

THE SHAPE OF GOD – PART I

So far, in thinking of God, we have been concerned with his character, so to speak, and have sought to answer our questions by
examining the character of man, who is created in his image. We
now have to raise problems of a slightly different nature: what is
God like to look at? how are we to imagine him? where does he live?

The Bishop of Woolwich begins *Honest to God* with the following words: 'The Bible speaks of a God "up there". No doubt its
picture of a three-decker universe, of "the heaven above, the earth
beneath and the waters under the earth", was once taken quite literally. No doubt also its more sophisticated writers, if pressed, would
have been the first to regard this as symbolic language to represent
and convey spiritual realities. Yet clearly they were not pressed.'

This clear-cut statement opens our eyes to a process that has been
going on throughout the ages. In any one generation, there is an
accepted scientific view of the universe. Men have always been
interested in the physical world and have discovered facts which they
could use to their advantage. Without this scientific curiosity, there
would have been no progress of any sort. Ancient scientists, though
differing in their methods and philosophy from our modern ones,
had this in common with them: that they sought out facts, tested
them as well as they were able, and developed theories in accordance
with them.

Thus, when the earliest writers thought of God as 'up there' in a
three-layered universe, they were reflecting the scientific notions of
their own day. It was, after all, a reasonable theory. The earth
looked flat and acted as if it were flat. There is no obvious reason
to suppose that you or I, if we had not been taught otherwise at
school, would think any differently. I once took part in a debate in
which I faced a science student who played the role of somebody
who thought the earth was flat. I was to prove that it was not. I
thought I had been given an easy task, but the science student won

the debate handsomely. He had plenty of facts, whereas my own faith in the 'roundness' of the world was based simply on believing what I had been told and accepting as adequate the slim evidence offered me at school.

At all events, once they assumed that the earth was flat, then it was obvious that the skies were up. When they dug down into the earth, they found moisture, and the lava which was flung up by volcanoes from underneath the earth was clearly not solid. So it was reasonable to talk of the moistures, or waters, that were under the earth.

And where, in a universe like this, was God imagined to live? Clearly in the sky. There had been previous generations which believed that he walked around on the earth like a man, or that he was to be found in stones and trees. But these views had gone. God was now seen, not as the inhabiter of an idol, a tree, a stream, or a mountain, but as a Spirit—everywhere. So his special dwelling place would be in the heavens and, if he came to earth, he would best be found in temples, tabernacles, and altars.

As time passed, knowledge of the universe increased and eventually the theory that the earth was flat was superseded. As this happened, it was natural that the old ideas should remain in the form of metaphor, image, or myth. This still goes on today. We talk of the sun 'rising' (though we know that it is the earth which goes round the sun); and it would be absurd if, in speaking of God, we pointed to the earth. Each time we refer to 'the sun rising' or raise our hands to the skies when we mention God, we know that we are using metaphors.

Unfortunately, religious people, anxious that God should be seen precisely, have often tried to make the theory of one age be accepted as an act of faith in a later age, when it could no longer be said to fit the facts.

We can see this in the familiar example of Adam and Eve and Evolution. The theory set out in chapter one of Genesis is an admirable one. It provides an explanation of the facts known to the writer and, in its expression, is full of sparkle and imagination. It describes an evolutionary process, starting with Light as the fundamental, seeing the first forms of life coming from water, and understanding man as the final product of the evolutionary process. In describing it, the writer had few precise facts. Not knowing how long each step in the process had taken, he talked of 'days'.

When, in the nineteenth century, new data were assembled, they were seen to produce very naturally the theory which we know popularly as Evolution. The theory, as Darwin himself tried to point out, in no way conflicted with belief in God and, in fact, simply stated more precisely what the Bible had stated vaguely. The Church reacted in a lamentable way. Bishop Wilberforce declared loudly that 'the principle of natural selection is absolutely incompatible with the word of God; if this thesis is true, Genesis is a lie, the whole framework of the book of life falls to pieces, and the revelation of God to man, as we Christians know it, is a delusion and a snare.' (Quoted by G. A. Coulson in *Science and Religion*.)

What nonsense! And how quickly we have seen that it *was* nonsense. Unfortunately, it was to Bishop Wilberforce that the majority of Christians listened, rather than to Darwin, though it should be remembered that Darwin's own supporters were, for the most part, Christian also.

What had happened? Bishop Wilberforce, instead of realizing that this is God's universe and therefore any discoveries about it are discoveries about God himself, had turned the scientific views of five thousand years earlier into an eternal and unchangeable statement of fact which, to disbelieve, meant atheism and a destruction of the word of God.

Again, we can do nothing about the past except to learn from it, and the new error may well be to elevate Darwin's ideas into a divine revelation for all times and places. The fact is that Darwin's theory remains a theory and will, in due time, be replaced by other, more sophisticated ones. It is to be hoped that, when this happens, Christians will not be found proclaiming the blasphemy of the new theories because they do not square with Darwin.

The idea that God lived 'up there' in a physical heaven, with a precisely described furniture, eventually departed and, as Bishop Robinson points out: 'in place of a God who is literally or physically "up there" we have accepted, as part of our mental furniture, a God who is spiritually or metaphysically "out there". For a while, men did not need to think very closely about this. The universe was so vast that God could easily be tucked into a part of it. Even though Christians had disposed of any literal belief in angels and principalities, thrones and heavenly choruses, they could still suppose that there was a heaven, and that God lived there.'

As scientists have probed more deeply into the Universe, however, it has become less possible to do this. No longer can we simply suppose that God may be fitted into those areas which Natural Science has left untouched. No longer can we look for gaps and say that God lives in them. God is the God of the whole Universe or he is not God at all. I find him, as Max Warren said, everywhere or I find him nowhere.

And I know that he does not live in the sky. In the test program for the new Parish Education Program, we set out a short incident for Junior Highs to discuss. It ran: 'When the Russian astronaut, Yuri Gagarin, returned from his orbit around the earth, he announced that he had seen no sign of God or the angels in space. But this did not seem to upset Christians. Why not? Should he have expected to see God in outer space?'

It came as no surprise to find that this section of the manual rated highly with teachers and students. For the problem was one with which they were familiar. They were not shattered by the Russian cosmonaut because they no longer believed that God occupied space; they certainly had no trouble in deciding that no bullet would hit him or even pass through him.

But where is he, then? When religious people moved from thinking about God as being 'up there' to a spirit 'out there', the leap was big enough, but the new one called for is greater and it has to be made in years instead of centuries. For, even when these previous leaps were made, God was still thought of as being someone outside man—a Highest Being. He was, in Robinson's words, 'a supreme Being, the grand Architect, who exists somewhere beyond the world —like a rich aunt in Australia—who started it all going, periodically intervenes in its running, and generally gives evidence of his benevolent interest in it.'

We are now asked to set such pictures aside for the moment. Our faith no longer demands that we consider God in this way at all. He need not be thought of as a Person who looks down on the world. He need not be thought of as one who, in order to live among us, had to come down and change his whole mode of behavior and life. He need not be thought of as a Being who exists apart from us and above us.

How, then, can we think of him? First of all, let us look back to the God of the Old Testament writers. Time after time we notice that he was presented in terms which matched their way of life. At first sight, it looks as though they were simply inventing a God in their own image; and so, in a sense, they were. But they were doing more than this. For they were not thinking of God simply as a reflection of a single way of life or a particular morality which they wished to perpetuate. Whenever they described him, it was as something ultimate in their lives. There was nothing more important, nothing beyond, nothing deeper, nothing higher.

Take, for example, the warrior God of the Old Testament. What was the situation? The Jews believed themselves to be the chosen race, picked out to advance mankind in a way which we now see to have been unique. The Jews are still unique, still in this sense the chosen race. The lead they give us in today's world is of the same quality as that given in the ancient world. It is a lead which embarrasses as well as it inspires; and it still produces opposition and persecution, even in the civilized metropolis cities of North America and Europe. It was necessary that they find a settled home for themselves and into this home they were led by Moses and succeeding leaders. The land they occupied was not uncivilized, the people who dwelt there were not heathen; they were an advanced race. What was the ultimate concern of the Jewish leaders? It was to occupy this land to the glory of God. Looking back, we can see that they might have chosen other ways, that there was no need to humiliate the Canaanites, that there was no final point established in smashing the Baals to pieces, and that the murdering of innocent women and children thwarted God's will rather than advanced it.

But we read the events with a great advantage. We have several thousands of years of new discoveries and we have had the Prophets and Christ to present man more brightly. Inasmuch as they expressed their ultimate concern, they were expressing God. They may have made the mistake, as we do, of following lesser concerns and allowing them to block the ultimate but, because they were dedicated to that beyond which there is no other, they were dedicated to God.

Or take the early Christian Church. What was their ultimate concern? What was it that they served beyond anything else? It was that they had met the living God and that nothing could ever again prevent the average man from doing the same. It was an old hope of the race to which these Christians belonged. It had reached an early climax when Moses tried to meet him but was put off by a burning bush. We shall never know why this happened as it did, nor why God would declare no more than '*I Am That I Am*'. It may have been that this was as far as Moses could go; it was his own ultimate.

At the back of his mind, built deep into his upbringing would be the belief that, if you know the name of a person you have power over him. The story of Rumpelstiltskin is a classic example of this old belief. Once the princess guessed the gnome's name, his power was gone, and he dashed his foot in anger through the floor. And you cannot have power over what is your ultimate concern, because then you yourself have become ultimate. But this is only guesswork. The facts are clear: Moses' God was his ultimate concern and was symbolized or represented or shown forth in the burning bush. The writer of this early story may well have been saying something like this when he indicated the limitations of Moses' position by suggesting that God showed to him only his backside.*

Now, in Jesus, God has been fully seen and touched and felt and listened to. And so his followers' ultimate concern is to know his resurrection. Nothing can replace this. It is beyond everything and includes everything. And so, though they try to escape martyrdom, they none the less accept it willingly when it comes. For their own lives are less than ultimate, and therefore they can surrender them.

In other words, God was their ultimate concern and Faith the unconditional demand made by their ultimate concern. Their Faith was an act of the whole personality and not simply a part of it. It took its place at the heart of their personal life and included all its elements. These, as I have it, are the conclusions reached by Paul Tillich in his *Systematic Theology* and his *Dynamics of Faith*.

The word God is a word which stands for my ultimate concern. There is nothing beyond it because then it would no longer be ultimate. I cannot fully understand it, because then my understanding would be ultimate.

It is by no means certain that I will serve my ultimate concern. I may, and often do, serve some concern within my easy grasp, and then I fall into idolatry. To take an example: there may be, ultimate in my life, Love. But I may, instead of Love, serve some lesser concern such as nationalism, religion, money, or status; and may even give my life to them. If I do so, I have served an idol. Or, I may replace the ultimate with myself. You may remember the old definition of Pride: putting oneself in the place of God. That is what happens when I replace the ultimate with myself.

---

*The metaphor, though picturesque, is not the most helpful.

CHAPTER EIGHT

THE SHAPE OF GOD – PART II

Paul Tillich has defined God as our 'Ultimate Concern' and, in doing so, offered us a description which can help many of us and ought not to hinder the others. At first sight, it seems a little cold, and we shall have to face this difficulty later in the chapter. But it does two things which, I think, are important: first, it liberates those Christians who have found the traditional portraits of God difficult, if not impossible, to accept. Second, it enables us to research new areas of man's life in the assurance that we shall make new discoveries about the infinite God.

Nor, so far as I can see, need this definition make life miserable for those who hold to traditional ideas. For, as we have seen, we can discover Tillich's definition within the definitions of those who wrote the Bible and formulated the Creeds. It includes everything which the traditional definitions included, but it opens up new lines of communication.

There is the same challenge to Faith. Tillich is not saying that we can plot God on a computer. Knowledge is not the Ultimate and we are still called on for the Leap of Faith which Karl Barth describes.

There is also an element of the Holy in Tillich's definition. In fact, he gives us back some of the old strength which lay in the word. For in the Old Testament, Holiness contained a marked element of the demonic as well as the godly: it was a terrifying thing as well as a comforting.

But Tillich also helps in areas where some of us find traditional theology weak. For example, it makes much clearer what is meant by doubt. We all know that doubt enters into every Christian's life. Tillich's definition implies that this doubt cannot be removed, and that it must be accepted with joy. This acceptance with joy he calls *courage*, not the word most of us would have thought of, but a convincing one all the same. In other words, the doubt which Tillich draws to our attention is not that of Saint Thomas (who was merely doubtful about a fact or a conclusion), but a doubt which is an *essential* element in Faith itself. It can be seen in the struggle which Jacob had with the angel; the fierce opposition of Moses to the tasks which lay ahead of him; the sweat pouring from Christ's brow as he resists the need to die; the denial of Peter; and the struggles of the saints with and against God ever since.

Tillich also helps us answer the question, so difficult to modern Christians: where does one find God? If he is a Being beyond me and outside me, I am limited in the areas where I can seek him, no matter how benevolently disposed he may be. For I am by definition lower than he is and therefore can only use myself to a minute extent in the search. It is true that traditional theologians are well aware of God's presence in all of us—they call it his *immanence*—but it is still a sort of condescension which is being described. The idea is still that God is 'out there', declaring, being, and on one occasion emptying himself into a human frame. Therefore, if I follow the traditional definitions and want to know more, I have to turn to 'metaphysics' (which thought things out from 'first principles' and produced the classical arguments for God's existence); and to 'authorities' (such as the Bible, the Church, bishops, the local rector, or Billy Graham). Unfortunately, the art of metaphysics is lost to us and no longer convinces; and we are becoming less inclined to accept anything simply on authority.

Tillich's definition opens the gates wide and does not even exclude an examination of metaphysics or the authorities. For, if God is my ultimate concern, then—although I cannot comprehend the ultimate —all areas of human experience lead me towards it. Once more we are led to the science of human relationships and the vision of God which has been opened up. When I look at myself, I find that I am not what I seem. I cannot fully understand myself, and need the help of others to appreciate even my most elementary and simple actions. When I look at others, I find myself in the presence of a new variety and depth which is beyond any final analysis, a depth of which I can only see the reflecting surface.

And then I consider the relationships between people. At this point, the imagination gives up as it always gives up when face to face with God. It is not that I am God, or you are God, or that our relationships with each other are God: it is that God, as our ultimate concern, is found, however much through a glass darkly, in persons.

Nor does this deny what is called the 'transcendence' of God, though it sets it in a different context from some earlier theologies. There is no suggestion here that God is limited to the discoveries we make about him when we examine ourselves; nor does it suggest that he has no existence independently of man. We may still accept the acts of Faith which perceive that God is more than the summing up of man's abilities and genius pressed to an infinite degree. Such acts of Faith are beyond any question valuable, for they create a response which is strong and freeing.

Yet the consequences of Tillich's discoveries are happy ones. In the past, the pressure has been to examine the 'unknown', that which is admittedly beyond our knowledge and grasp. As I have just suggested, this is still not denied to us. But we may now see the value of examining what we actually have in front of us. It is more than enough, for there is clearly no chance that we will ever fully comprehend the variety in nature and especially in ourselves.

A few lines above, I used the word 'depth'. It is a favorite word with Tillich and Bishop Robinson. It is also a good one. For, as Robinson points out, we are much concerned with the depth of life. 'Up in the sky' does not convey anything like as powerful a message as 'deep'. For even the probing of space and the working out of unlimited universes can only take place because the men who do the probing are infinite in possibility.

This message was brought home to us by the Incarnation. Here the traditional descriptions of God, though a help to previous generations and to many today, are now a hindrance to many others. There was a time when Christians imagined God to inhabit the vast space of the sky. At a certain point in the story of mankind, he decided to become man, and was born to Mary. In Saint Paul's vivid metaphor: he emptied himself, taking the form of a man.

As soon as Christians began to think about this birth, there came into being the great problems of early theology. How can we reconcile Christ's humanity with his divinity? Did God live side by side with a human Jesus like two crabs living inside a single shell? Was his godhead the real thing, his humanity simply a cloak for it? Was his humanity the principal factor, and his divinity a gift which he earned by his great goodness? When God came to earth, what did he leave in heaven? When Jesus prayed to God, was he praying to himself?

These, and other problems, remain to haunt those who have to deal with such people as Jehovah's Witnesses.

The Church's traditional answers to such questions consisted of certain key statements. Christ was divine. Christ was human. Though both human and divine, he was one person. There are two other persons who are also God: the Father and the Holy Ghost. They are three separate persons; yet there is only one God.

These statements were a fair enough challenge to faith and, within the areas set by the scientific knowledge of the day, a sufficient answer. A man knows that his mind is not the same as his body, and neither are the same as his soul; and yet he knows himself to be one. This was not an exact parallel, but it showed that the Church's interpretation of the Incarnation was a good one.

Thanks to a growing insight into God's creation and therefore his being, and thanks to such definitions as that of Tillich, we are freed from these problems. (Though we have created some new ones, of course.) We need no longer imagine God as a grand super-being pouring himself into a human shell. We no longer have to go out into space to gain an idea of the infinity and immortality of God and his creation. When Jesus declared, 'The Kingdom of Heaven is within you', the statement may have meant very little to his hearers, but it comes through powerfully to us today.

Thanks to the analyses of personality which followed the initial work of Freud, we can now face certain facts without fear. We can accept the idea that we are all imperfect. We can see that motives are not only obscure but beyond complete analysis; that the pious doctrines of the faithful have no more guarantee of truth than the beliefs of others; that the motivation of religious thinkers is as uncertain as that of their enemies. We can see that the distinction between the faithful and the heretic is as intolerable to God as that between Jew and Samaritan. We are all under judgement, and the fervent Christian who declares the doom of the pagan is wasting his energy. The difference between the holiest Pope and the most irresponsible bum is negligible. For the first time in history, we can say without shame or guilt, that 'when we have done all, we are still unprofitable servants.' If Freud and his followers have taught us nothing else, we can thank them for showing us clearly that the first is last and the last first.

When we think of Christ, we think of a perfect man. He is exactly as we are, in all ways, except that there is no gap between what he is and what he might be. He is without sin. When he challenges us to follow him, he is challenging us to follow on the same road he treads, which is the road we are actually on. When he tells us to be perfect as God is perfect, he is offering a possibility which exists in the way of life we know, not a different or higher way.

One of the problems posed by Tillich, however, must be faced squarely. How does one draw or paint an ultimate concern, or sing hymns of praise to it, or write cantatas and anthems? The fact is that one cannot do so at all.

But there is no reason why one should. Those of you who did mathematics at school will remember how often, when you compiled some new and more comprehensive system of numbers, the old ones were somehow built into it. So it is with our new descriptions and portraits of God. They do not carry on the old, nor do they destroy it. They fulfil it, in the same way that Jesus' radical changes fulfilled the former Law. What is valuable remains. The baby is not thrown out with the bath water: he is simply rescued from drowning.

And one of the things which remains is the old imagery. When I think of God, I think of a large man in a flowing robe with a beard, and I see no reason to change this. I know that it is not a literal fact; I know it is a metaphor, or a parable, or a myth, or whatever label you care to use. When I sing hymns, I see no reason why I should give up the saints casting down their golden crowns around the glassy sea. I cannot imagine what possible purpose this can have served, but it conjures up a vision of brightness, joy and carelessness which is, for me, a consequence of accepting Tillich's definition.

CHAPTER NINE

CHURCH WORSHIP

We have been talking in the past few chapters about the Shape of God—what he is like. This shape is known to us in Worship and, in fact, the word gives us a clue to this. It comes from two Old English words, the first of which resembled our word *worth* and meant *value*, the second of which became our modern suffix *-ship* (as in scholar-*ship*) and meant *shape*. The whole word meant literally 'the shape of being the good' or, in our present context, the Shape of God.

In other words, it is in Worship that we find God.

As soon as we say this, we can see that Worship has a much wider and deeper meaning than simply being in Church going through prayers and actions. For God is everywhere, in all people, and at all times. He is not, as we have discovered, boxed up, nor can he be boxed up, in a church building, or anywhere else. Wherever we meet God, we worship him; and we meet him everywhere. Worship lies in the shake of a hand, the wink of an eye, the quick walk, the exchanged word, in the street, the home, the dance hall and church.

It is important that we look closely at what we do in church. For if we are losing sight of God in our Services, rather than seeking him; if we are excluding the world rather than finding it built into every ritual and ceremony; then we are excluding God from the very activity which is supposed to discover what he is like.

These questions are asked very frequently nowadays: is our Church Worship leading us to God or away from him? Is it helping us find ourselves at one with him, or is it encouraging a way of thought and life which separates us?

As soon as I set these simple questions down on paper, I realize that there is a great obstacle. How many readers, for example, have already felt uneasy, that the above questions are verging on the irreverent? For, strange as it may seem in the twentieth century, the Services we hold in church are somehow thought of as above or beyond criticism.

Early in 1964, I took part in a parish discussion group. Excellent progress had been made during the previous meetings and, when we came to look at the worship of the congregation on Sunday morning, the rector and I anticipated that we would be in for some exciting thought.

The meeting was exciting enough, but most of the excitement led us away from the Prayer Book, and from any realistic examination of our Worship. It became clear that the group, well above average in intelligence and filled with less fear than most, had shirked the issue. To our surprise, the flight from an examination of Church Worship took place at the moment we opened the Prayer Book with a view to discussing possible changes. One or two members considered that this was essentially the work of the bishops and clergy and that, once passed by General Synod, the Prayer Book had the same sort of authority as the Bible, and should not be questioned by mere laymen.

Here then is a call for a change in our attitude to which it will not be easy to adjust ourselves. It is a strange tragedy that we are most afraid to look frankly at the very part of our life which we believe to be crucial; and, in producing this unwillingness, I am as much to blame as anyone. For years, I used to preach that, give or take a few details, the Worship of the Church had reached its highest point in 'our incomparable Liturgy', and that congregations need only understand its shape and logic to feel its great excitement. As time passed, it became obvious that this excitement was not reflected in the conduct of the congregation. So I worked harder at trying to be exciting. When young people informed me that they found the whole thing boring, instead of being pleased at their honesty, I rushed to the defence of the Services in order to show that, in spite of outward appearances, they were all really very wonderful underneath.

I have heard many other clergy describe the same rat race of trying to persuade themselves and their congregations that a little care, faith, or knowledge about the shape of Holy Communion and Morning Prayer would soon show how relevant, important, and alive they are.

The biggest criticism came, not from the lips of the young people, but their actions and those of their elders. Very few adults admitted to boredom and many of them insisted that they found everything fine. Only a few were willing to discuss the matter at all. Yet, all over the western world, the majority of people no longer attended church regularly, and found that the most superficial reasons for absenteeism were accepted by themselves, their families and the clergy.

Behind all this lay a simple point which few would face. We had assumed that, if the Services seemed boring or meaningless, the people must be at fault, and more care or faith would help them rise to the high level of word and action set out in the Prayer Book. There was, however, another solution. The boredom might be justified. The Services might have become remote and, in the twentieth century, have little meaning. They might simply be a shell of the liveliness of a previous generation, now only helpful to those who wanted to escape from contemporary life into the warmth of a more distant way of speech and action.

In the modern Liturgical Movement, men of nearly every denomination are struggling to discover the nature of this modern malaise. It would be rash to imply that any firm answers have been reached, but the progress made since the beginning of this century has been impressive. Perhaps the biggest contribution made has been to identify the sort of questions we ought to be asking ourselves, for the biggest step is to acknowledge that the questions are legitimate and that, though answers will be long in coming (and may not be justified in any case), the questions must continue in greater number and depth. There is nothing which justifies us in accepting a Liturgy uncritically, for it should never be a prison in which we expect to snare the living God.

Here are some of the questions we may well ask ourselves:

1. Are people excited by the Worship of the Church? Some say yes, some no. We can take their word for this and acknowledge that we are divided on the question. We would be wise, however, to note that a cold or difficult day often means a small congregation; and that the greatest numbers of people select Christmas and Easter (with their color, sing-able hymns and warmer atmosphere) as the occasions when they attend Church. We might occasionally observe the nodding heads, the glazed eyes and the impatient wriggling of children.

2. To those who find the Services adequate: are you willing to agree that many people do not? that those who do not attend church

are often very good people? and that they may find our Services dead and remote? There are people who attend church regularly who wish to see great changes made in the Prayer Book. Have they a right to this feeling? or do you think they are being misled? There are many clergy who are beginning to experiment with the worship services. Do you think that they ought to be encouraged? or do you think they are disloyal and should be told to stop?

3. To those who are unhappy with the present situation: what sort of changes do you wish? Is there a danger of simply replacing a dead form of words with a set of superficial gimmicks?

4. To those who feel that this is not a widespread problem and that what has been written so far is an expression of an unusual, radical, or oddball point of view: have you examined the careful researches made into the subject? These researches, mostly in the United States and England, conclude in every case that church worship is seen by most people as unreal.

5. There are leading Christian writers who insist that there is a close relationship between Liturgy and Work, and that we have made a tragic error in separating them. What do you think about this? and do you think that our Services encourage us to separate worship from the rest of our life? If you want to examine this subject more deeply, make a point of buying John Kirby's outstanding *The Kingdom, the Power, and the Glory*.

6. Do you think the clergy dominate worship too much? In an excellent paper on *Worship*, Clarke Raymond writes: 'I always felt I had to be hearty and push along in the psalms, as if the whole tone depended on what I did. When the choir moved to the gallery, I felt terribly alone and conspicuous in my fancy dress, but I wonder if it is any less a one-man show when shielded by a choir. Just the sheer number of words which the priest says in the course of Mattins or in the Eucharist makes it seem as if the people are just coming along for the ride. I can remember big discussions about whether the layman who was going to read the epistle should wear a white surplice or not, as if the leader had to be almost a clergyman, or at least look like one. In my first parish there was a terrible row because ordinary laymen did the job of the vested server in bringing the bread and wine to the altar. So I'm not blaming anyone but just pointing out how

dominant is the role and appearance of the clergyman in worship. It even moves over into a confirmation, where the congregation becomes confused as to which deserves more attention, the class of newly confirmed or the bishop. Even the reception seems to centre about the bishop. The strangeness of this has something to do with having to be a patriarch in a non-patriarchal society.'*

Two adjustments called for, then, are an acknowledgement that questioning the Liturgy is legitimate and desirable; and that it will take a long time to discover an adequate definition of Worship. The two provisional definitions offered by Clarke Raymond will, I think, help start much discussion:

1. Worship is an act which reflects and summarizes the life of the community which engages in it. 'From such a point it is possible to look at parish life and enquire whether the Eucharist is the typical act of this community or whether a bazaar is more appropriate.'

2. Worship is the celebration of the presence and activity of God in the world. Here is an example: 'The local Golf Club has extended the privilege of membership beyond the old limits of prejudice. Here is an indication of the presence and activity of God in the world which our liturgy ought to celebrate.'

Behind, alongside, or contained in public worship is private prayer. In *Honest to God*, John Robinson tells of a moment in his life when he began to know a real freedom. 'I have not forgotten the relief with which twenty years ago, back at my theological college, I discovered in a conversation of the small hours a kindred spirit, to whom also the whole of the teaching we received on prayer meant little. There was nothing about it one could say was wrong. Indeed, it was an impressive roundabout; but one was simply not on it—and, what was worse, had no particular urge to be. To realize that after all one might not be the chief of sinners, or the only man out of step, lifted a load of secret, yet basically unadmitted guilt.'

You will notice that we have here the same basic problem we are

*This paper, which sets out several other problems and some of the answers being sought in the modern Church, may be obtained from the Department of Religious Education, 600 Jarvis Street, Toronto 5, Ont.

meeting throughout this book: that, faced with an uncomfortable feeling that the traditional teachings leave us less than warm, our first reaction is to feel guilty and to think that, somehow or other, a little more faith or work will make them seem better, more convincing, or truer. It is only later, if at all, that it occurs to us that the teachings may no longer be appropriate *for us today*. We make here no criticisms of former generations. They had different lives to lead. They had different problems. They were faced with sudden death and suffering every minute of their lives, especially at night. If they were poor, they had no rights, and the immorality of their rulers had to be accepted as a cruel fact of life, declared by the same rulers to be the will of God. It is no surprise to find that the forms of teaching enshrined, for example, in the Catechism, could be used effectively, and for a wide variety of reasons. The question is whether, in our much changed society, the basic assumptions and methods of the Catechism do, or do not, make teaching difficult or impossible.

Many people are in the position in which John Robinson found himself. If they consider their lives alongside the patterns offered in devotional books, sermons and the Catechism, they have to admit: 'I just don't know how to pray.' They then go on to wish that they could be like the rector or the visiting missioner or somebody. The man in the next pew looks very reverent with his closed eyes: he probably prays more deeply than I do. It would not be difficult.

And then one day the great discovery is made. I have taken part in many groups in which, step by step, with slow fearful progress, a dozen people have found themselves looking at each other in a new light. I remember a woman breaking down into almost uncontrollable sobbing: 'I thought I was the only one who couldn't pray.' And then the sudden tidal wave of relief and freedom from a guilt which need never have been. During the next five minutes, no words were spoken, though I noticed many drumming fingers and oscillating adam's apples; and, in myself, a hollow feeling. On leaving, a man said, 'That was the first time in my life I prayed.' It may well have been the last, but one such prayer torn out of the depths of life's sadness and nonsense may be worth a million routines of ordered offices.

On the other hand, it may not. It is no part of this book to criticize

those who find the traditional methods a genuine help. It is, however, its part to suggest that men are made in the image of God and
not books, creeds, or devotional aids. Those who enjoy or benefit
from the 'five points in prayer'* are to be supported completely and
not criticized in any way. The problem of the present age is to discover how to help those who find the five points useless or nearly
useless; who cannot conceive in any way what is meant by 'adoration'; who go through a form of confession without the remotest
idea of what it means to be forgiven in the midst of their often
church-created guilt; and who, desperately needing others and wanting to help them, cannot see much relationship between this and
what is glibly called Intercession.

A rapidly growing number of Christians are saying, with Bishop
Robinson: 'We do not find them much help.' What is the attitude of
the Church to be? Are we to say that the critics are unjustified and
small in number? that everything is all right under the surface?
Are we to hope that the problem will go away soon and that the
people will return to loving the present Prayer Book language and
the older forms of prayer? Are we to feel that the men and women
who hold such views are wrong and should be reprimanded?

My own view must be obvious. I think that we have to go on
offering the 'five points' (and the rest of the roundabout) to those
who can use them, still a fair number of people. But we have to
spend much more of our time trying to understand those who cannot use them, and discover in what new directions God may be
leading us. There is a changed atmosphere and we cannot escape it.

---

*Adoration, Thanksgiving, Petition, Confession, and Intercession.

CHAPTER TEN

THE CHURCH AND SCIENCE

God is the God of all life. If this is so, then he is the God of Science also and in Science we will find him at work as clearly as in the Church. He will reveal himself in the laboratory as he does in the sanctuary and the discoveries of scientists will be as much discoveries of God as are the researches of theologians.

This is common sense. And yet such simple statements as these can cause difficulty, not only in Church circles, but among outsiders as well. The fact is that many people distinguish between 'churchmen' and 'scientists', and between 'religion' and 'science'.

In 1961, Maclean's Magazine published a report by Ralph Allen on research in Guelph, Ontario. They asked certain questions to test whether Church members were much influenced by the views of their Church. In answer to the question: *Can you think of anything you did in the past year as a direct result of Church influence?*— 19% of Protestants said '*Yes*'; 81% said '*No*'; 11% of Roman Catholics said '*Yes*'; 89% said '*No*'. This was followed up by a more detailed question, the results of which were recorded as follows:

Question: *Has your behaviour been specifically affected in any of the following matters as a result of Church attendance?*

(Percentage who said '*Yes*')	Protestants	Roman Catholics
Use of alcohol	11.4	3
Birth control	5	21
Sunday observance	25	17
Sexual behaviour	2.5	11
Political decisions	6.6	3
Public causes or organisations	12.5	14
Business or professional conduct	20	6

This did not come as a surprise to those of us who had worked

49

in parishes for a quarter of a century. Much lip-service is paid, of course, but it is only an individual here and there who makes a major decision in terms of the demands he feels his Church is making. Most people distinguish between the Church and the rest of life and the predominant influence is not the Church.

Some years ago, I did a stint of work for an English professional polling organisation. My job was to interview a cross-section of the population and ask them about twenty to twenty-four questions. One or two of these asked whether the person interviewed recognized some trade name or advertizing slogan; and the answers paid most of the cost of the research. The rest were concerned with the usual matters raised in Gallup surveys. The only difference, so far as my own work was concerned, was that, having completed the interview for which I was paid, I added a few questions of my own choosing. The results were inadequate, but none the less provided some interesting data.

I have the figures still. Out of two hundred and thirty people approached over a period of one year, I found nobody at all who thought the Church influenced the nation's life in any way, except that the archbishop crowned the monarch. What about individual lives? Here there was less unanimity, but only seventeen expressed any real connection between what they did and the views of the Church. The norm could well be represented in the phrase 'Well— not really'. One reply, in my opinion, summed up the general response to perfection: 'I'd like to, cock, but wot abaht the bloody parsons?' He wouldn't want to stand in the way of the missus, however.

As to where those interviewed felt the real source of modern progress and life lay, there was no doubt. The answer came from all denominations: it was Science. To forty people, I posed the question: '*Do you think God works through scientists?*' and received '*Don't know*' from thirty-seven, '*No*' from two, and '*Yes*' from one who said he had a brother who worked in a research laboratory.

This general response was echoed in every parish with which I was connected. I remember, as typical, a Mission held during Lent in a thickly populated parish south of the River Thames. One of the questions which I constantly asked of a wide variety of people during the Mission was: '*Who do you feel you can respect?*' The answer was, for the most part, '*nobody*'. But a grudging nod was made in the direction of the scientists. They were, I was told, clever at any rate, though they were still after the main chance and might blow us all up. Clergy? If ever I had any delusions as to our reputation with the public, they departed abruptly when I was answered.

There was an even subtler embarrassment. For a moment, the people of whom I had asked the question about the clergy had clearly forgotten (or half-forgotten) that I was a priest. It was sad to notice how, suddenly realizing it, some of the group deserted honesty and tried to soften the blow. When I reflected on the incident afterwards, I realized that I had been very pleased to be taken for a layman.

In the popular view, the Church and Science are separated as distinct entities. This unspoken assumption comes out in parts of Pierre Berton's *The Comfortable Pew*. He states, for example: 'The atheists, agnostics, Unitarians, socialists, and scientists were all on record before the major organized Christian community.' But this is a strange list. It is as though he had said that meat, oranges, and candy tasted better than fruit. For the 'major organized Christian community' contains scientists. Many of them are members of congregations; some of them are clergy.

Yet Berton's implication is understandable. Moreover, the popular assumption goes further. Not only are Religion and Science thought of as separate and distinct, but they are thought of as enemies. It is still widely assumed that Religion is at war with Science and that a good churchman must be suspicious, if not at loggerheads with, any scientist. It is a mystery how this idea can survive in the face of leading scientists who are Christian, but it does survive, and we have to ask why.

It survives, I think, because, though the Victorian struggles are over, they are not completely dead. This was shown dramatically when the United Church of Canada brought out its admirable New Curriculum. In these materials, the writers made it plain that there were many stories in the Bible which were, like the Prodigal Son, offered to bring out an important truth. They need not be taken as history. Particular cases quoted were the early stories of Genesis. The reaction of most Church members and Sunday School teachers was quick and definite: they were relieved to hear that the Church at last acknowledged officially what they themselves had been feeling most of their lives. But there were fairly large numbers of people who were unwilling to recognize this, and who demonstrated by their letters to the newspapers and the *United Church Observer*, that the old fight is still alive. That this cannot be dismissed lightly on the grounds that opponents to change in the Church are born 'writers to the editor' can be seen when we note that the Baptist Church was about evenly divided on the issue and that many of its local congregations have refused to use the new material on the grounds that it teaches such passages as the early parts of Genesis to be parable or myth.*

The assumption that there is a barrier between Religion and Science is kept alive by other than fundamentalist Christians. Very often the biggest opposition towards change in the Church comes from people who have left. As John Robinson points out, 'This is not an attractive proposition: it will be resented by most unthinking non-churchgoers, who tend to be more jealous of the beliefs they have rejected and deeply shocked that they should be betrayed.'

Thus, it is clear that the modern Church, due to a greatly increased sensitivity, is willing to accept and listen to criticism. This gives opponents a field day and most of them show great charity and a desire to help the Church come to terms with reform. But it is not true of all opponents. It sometimes appears as though the non-Christian is anxious that the Church should stay backward, remaining heavily different from the rest of society; and will block any attempts made by the Church to change. I find this difficult to comprehend, unless it is that a conventional, conservative Church is one which the outsider can reject with a clear conscience. Put another way: if the Church were to come alive in the second part of the twentieth century, it would be just as difficult to be an agnostic as it is now to be a Christian.

---

*There is an interesting sideline to this. In the past, when a piece of dogma has been discarded, it has often been replaced by another. The fundamentalist dogmas concerning the Old Testament myths have now nearly gone, but we seem to be in danger of replacing them with new ones. Our present scientific theories concerning the origin of life may well be radically modified or even overturned in the future; and it may be that those who support this change will be shouted down by the same type of person who first resisted Darwin. Dogmatism is never far away from us, whether it is declared in the name of science, agnosticism, Unitarianism or Christianity. It is always a sign of unreality and often of fear, even when it happens by coincidence to express a truth.

At all events, whatever the reasons, the facts are inescapable. Take a daily newspaper and look for the pages which deal with the Church. There are odd exceptions, such as a column by Archbishop Pocock but, for the most part, Church news is tucked away into a ghetto filled with ecclesiastical symbols, jostled by horrible little advertisements for Church Services. Or examine the way radio and television station programs deal with Church matters. Once more, they are pushed away into a little corner which says loudly to the listener that the broadcasting industry (not, in this case, the Church) regards religion as something on the side. In *The Comfortable Pew*, Pierre Berton very skilfully draws attention to the Church's own shortcomings in this regard, but the attempts by the Church to correct this are often cold-shouldered, as for example when Mr. Berton himself criticises the Stan Freberg spots without analysing the sociological findings of the researchers.

Moreover, it seems that the news media are anxious to keep the whole arena of debate back in the nineteenth century. Towards the end of 1964, Mr. Aubrey Wice of the Toronto *Telegram* visited the Reverend Philip Jefferson, the man largely responsible for the development of our new curriculum materials. The prime aim of these materials is to help teachers free themselves from some of the difficulties they have formerly experienced and to move easily and flexibly with their students. Mr. Jefferson pointed out that we were not particularly concerned with the Genesis-myth-Darwin problems which the United Church had encountered, and in fact did not raise the issue strongly in our materials. We were more concerned with helping the teachers and students to come to terms with the under-lying beliefs. Yet, when Mr. Wice appeared in print, the main part of Mr. Jefferson's new and revolutionary thinking was suppressed and the limelight cast on the hoary old Victorian struggle over *Genesis*, which had occupied Mr. Jefferson for very little time and then only in response to repeated questions. This is not to complain about Mr. Wice's article as such, because he is a first class reporter and is likely reflecting a policy of giving the public what the editors feel the public wants; but it certainly demonstrates that the problems of the Church, as it tries to move into the twentieth century, are not just the product of sluggish thinking on the part of its members, but also of blocking from outside.

Bearing in mind, then, that the old dividing lines between Religion and Science are not yet obliterated, we can none the less come to terms with a few direct suggestions. In the first place, the Church, as an institution, was wrong in its fight with Darwin and his successors, and came out of the nineteenth century looking very foolish. At almost every point where issue was joined between the institutional Church and Science, the views of the latter were to be proven and accepted by the vast majority of mid-twentieth century Christians. This needs to be stated without qualification, because it opens up an important question: to whom does God reveal himself and who listens to him? So far as the narrow nineteenth century struggle between Bishop Wilberforce and the British Association was concerned, God was revealing himself to both, but it was the latter who heard him, rather than the former.

At the Anglican Congress, the new role of the Church was presented vigorously by John Lawrence.* Thinking of the whole area of secular life, which includes the scientific, he stated forthrightly: 'It is the task of the Church in this age to proclaim that the secularists have been right in their revolt, but wrong in the conclusions that they draw from it. The Church herself should proclaim the autonomy from ecclesiastical control of art, science, politics, business and other secular concerns; at the same time she should proclaim the sovereignty of God over these concerns, a sovereignty that is exercised in more ways than we expect to know.' So far as Science is concerned, we must see clearly, state clearly, and act clearly that we come as servants, not as masters.

It is now, perhaps, necessary to spell out a little of what this means for us. So far, we have been looking in effect at what was a power struggle between the institutional Church and institutional Science, a struggle in which we can, without fear, admit that the former was in error. But the institutional Church does not stand for all its members. Even at the height of Bishop Wilberforce's ridiculous posturing, there were churchmen who supported Darwin and, before and since, many who have given important aid in scientific research.

We can, therefore, feel confident as we see the modern Church coming out of hiding and taking a frank look at Science, knowing that God is working through it. We have no need to be on the defen-

*John Lawrence is the editor of the magazine *Frontier*.

sive, to hang on to the tatters of previous convictions, or to feel it necessary to be the ones who declare while others listen.

Above all, we have no need to look around for areas of life where we can still say: 'Here, at least, religion carries more power than science.' This sort of last-ditch resistance is sometimes found today, and the God it sets up is often known as the 'God of the gaps'. It declares that we see religion as that area of life about which Science does, or can, make no firm pronouncements. But this is an abominable suggestion. If I say that we should let scientists deal with material things whilst the Church deals with spiritual, I am suggesting that there is some fundamental difference between the two, and implying that God's material creation is not spiritual, and that the things of the spirit are not available for scientific examination.

If I accept this distinction, I will find that, as the years pass, wider and wider areas of life are passing into the keeping of the scientists and smaller areas left to the Church. I remember a Rector once preaching with great eloquence that we walk, as it were, to the edge of a great cliff. All behind us is the landmass known as Science. Ahead of us is the bright land of Truth. But the two are separated by a deep canyon across which we have to jump. 'That jump,' he declared, 'is the jump of Faith.' Unfortunately the cliff seems to get larger, and it seems less necessary to jump.

This is intolerable. I am every bit as human as a scientist and the whole of life is as much my concern as it is his, just as God is as much revealed to him as to me. We are saying, therefore, that any distinction between Religion and Science which implies that the one or the other comes closer to God, is false. The truth is that Science is a religious exercise in itself. It is of no importance whether or not the scientist recognizes this. So far as the Church is concerned, the scientist is seeking the truth and seeking it, so far as is humanly possible, with a minimum of prejudice. He is, therefore, seeking God.

When we have made this step, it is not very difficult to make the next. For, in the modern world, the methods used by Science to discover the truth are very good ones and can be used by theologians.

At the risk of over-simplifying, I think we might look at it this way. The scientist starts off with the assumption that whatever he finds to be true must be accepted until somebody provides a different or more accurate answer. Having put forward a theory which he feels meets the facts, he then tests it remorselessly and expects other people to do the same. Some scientists have fallen into the trap of declaring themselves infallible and resisting those who have criticized them, but they form a minority. It is the expectation of most scientists that their theories will one day be superseded by more accurate ones. The great Michael Faraday summed this up: 'Though I cannot honestly say that I *wish* to be found in error, yet do I fervently hope that the progress of science in the hands of the many zealous cultivators will be such as, by giving us new and other developments, and laws more and more general in their application, will make even me think that what is written and illustrated in these experimental researches, belongs to the by-gone parts of science.'

Here is the meekness which Jesus said would inherit the earth, a true humility which is found only rarely in theology. For in theology we often meet a quite different assumption—the assumption that, somewhere along the line, God has declared himself firmly in such a way that the words and ideas may never be improved. Very often, when a religious thinker questions the Creed, or the Catechism, he is quickly accused of deserting the faith 'once for all delivered to the saints'. Here is theological conceit at its crudest. For the saints were no more accurate or faithful in their lives and thinking than those who succeeded them and, with the meekness of Faraday, may very well have hoped that, though their doctrines be not proved in error, the day might come when they would rejoice to see their Creeds superseded by better ones.

We are not infallible. Yet temptations to claim infallibility are very strong. If only we believe that the Pope, or the Bible, or the General Synod speaks the word of God and that we may not question it, then we are very happy people. But it does not work, and we are very well aware that it does not. The infallible oracle inevitably declares some hard fact which a later generation disputes and disproves. We live in an uncertain world, and we have to live uncertainly.

CHAPTER ELEVEN

DENOMINATIONS

One of the prisons in which man has tried to restrain God is the denomination. The underlying assumption here is that God is to be found only, or best, in a certain branch of the Christian Church, or even a party within that branch. It was an assumption often made in the past, and is not completely dead today. The classical example is the Roman Catholic Church which, until recently, claimed to be the one true Church, all others being described as separated or heretical. The other Churches saw the error of Rome's ideas very clearly and protested loudly against the exclusive tone of her pronouncements; but this did not prevent them making the same assumption, even when they did not declare it officially. Protestant denominations, equally with Rome, have implied that God would find himself most at home in certain Churches, or types of Church. At home—or, as we now see it, in prison.

The position taken by the Anglican Church was one which fascinated other denominations and often repelled them. Attacking strongly the narrow ideas of Rome, we imitated her when we came to deal with those parts of Christendom which we called 'Protestant'. I don't think that we ever claimed officially that God was incapable of working outside the Anglican Church, but we often acted as if we did. The orders of Methodist ministers were cheerfully pronounced invalid, their sacraments to be avoided by good Anglicans, and they themselves kept away from our altars. When we came to our own position, we were quick to describe what we fondly imagined was a bridge church. In short, we made—and were clearly seen by others to make—an assumption of superiority.

Within the Anglican Church there also used to exist what we may call splinter denominations, united in their acceptance of a common Prayer Book, a common ministry, and certain ways of behaving and organizing themselves. Outside of this, however, the divisions were marked and strong. The Low Church party saw themselves

57

acting not only differently from others, but somehow better. The High Church party did not consider themselves an expression of a different mood or feeling in the worship of God, but a purer body within the one, true, holy, Catholic and apostolic church. So deep were the assumptions of superiority that there are Canadian towns which still have a church specifically built to represent one party or the other and, in the metropolis of Toronto, a wry reminder in the continued separate existence of Wycliffe and Trinity Colleges.

Fortunately, although pockets of continued tension still survive, the old denominational exclusiveness has departed. The situation as we face Rome is quite different from what it was even ten years ago. Soon after his ascent to the papal throne, the late John XXIII made it clear that he would lead his Church into the new age. His early pronouncements were not particularly revolutionary, but the atmosphere was. When, therefore, the Vatican Council came to meet, one of the big issues which faced the Roman Church was: what is our attitude to those who are not Roman Catholics? Whatever might be the official legal statements, there was no escaping the fact that the Pope regarded Protestants and Jews as friends, and that the idea of heresy was probably doomed.

The relaxation of tension at the local level was immediate. No longer are Jews dismissed into the heathen recesses of life where they may be spat on;* no longer are Protestants to be treated as unbelievers and the followers of antichrist, but separated brethren and, it seems in some local circumstances, brethren. No longer can prayers only be thought acceptable to God when taken by a Roman Catholic, but common prayers are becoming frequent and the areas in which they seem legitimate are constantly becoming larger.

*There may be exceptions. Mr. L. Denis Byrne (an Anglican) in the December 1964 issue of the *Canadian Churchman*, writes: 'We are told very definitely by Arnold Edinborough that we Anglicans must quit praying for the conversion of the Jewish people on Good Friday. Apparently we must recognize that had they not rejected our Blessed Lord and had their priesthood not brought about his crucifixion, God's purpose would not have been fulfilled. Therefore, in continuing to reject Christ, they are worshipping God in a way which we Christians should recognize, and we should make no attempt to proselytize them. Evidently we are expected to concede that Christ was specifically excluding the Jews when he said, "They who are not for me are against me". And again: "Except ye eat the flesh of the Son of Man and drink his blood, ye have no life in you." And: "I am the way, the truth and the life; no man cometh unto the Father, but by me." '

The attitude of denominations other than Rome has changed radically. When the Church of South India was first formed, there was much anxiety and many Anglicans stated that members of the new body should not be admitted to communion in our Churches. Fortunately, this strange attempt to box God up did not become widespread, and a turning point came when the 'High Church' Society for the Propagation of the Gospel, unable to use its funds to help the workers in the Church of South India, set up a special fund to which its subscribers could contribute and which would be used for the new Church. Since then, the atmosphere has altered completely and opponents of the South Indian experiment are now very few.

Discussions between different denominations are constantly occurring. Name any two and there are probably unity conversations going on at this moment. So far as the official approaches of the Church are concerned, there is a new feeling altogether. At the 1963 meetings of the Executive Council at Banff, the Committee discussing unity with the United Church was given a strong supporting arm from the whole assembly and encouraged to do a complete piece of work. More important, perhaps, was the atmosphere in which the discussion was conducted. Whenever, in the past, I have been present at debates on Union, at least one speaker has quoted Saint Thomas, made references to the 'Catholic Faith' or urged the dangers of hobnobbing with Protestantism. At Banff, the atmosphere was one of support and a straightforward feeling that, if General Synod played cold feet again, it would be a matter of shame for the whole Anglican Church.

Such discussions are constantly recurring and I think it would be fair to say that, with the exception of the sects and some individual people within the major denominations, it is now accepted that the various denominations should come together. This Unity is not defined very closely and there are many who would be unhappy with a Uniformity which might enclose us in a new, though bigger, prison. The accepted opinion is there, however, and at the parish level most congregations are convinced that there should be Unity.

Problems remain, none the less. In the first place, though a happy atmosphere may prevail when we are talking generally about 'healing our alarming divisions', it can be broken by the first practical suggestion. In a letter to *The National Catholic Reporter*, George Lewis

—one of Canada's leading writers in the field of Anglican-Roman Catholic relationships—wrote: 'As an Anglican married to a truly progressive-minded Roman Catholic, I have some experience in practical ecumenism on a round-the-clock basis. My wife and I are, as you can imagine, desperately concerned to hasten the day when Anglican and Roman Catholic Christians can meet together *as they should* where it really counts—namely, at Our Lord's Table in the sharing of His holy Body and Blood.' It is in the communion that our sincerity is tested.

In a Questionnaire sent out to Anglican Clergy in the Spring of 1964, the Department of Religious Education was anxious to test how far down the road we had come towards a practical re-union. We wanted to know, first of all, what general steps were being taken and whether the Anglican clergy met frequently at meetings with the clergy of other denominations. We asked, therefore: *During the past year, have you met with clergy of other denominations to discuss or act upon common problems?* To this question 199 responded *Yes*, 40 *No*, 8 gave no answer, and 73 made no comments. In general, most of the people who met with other clergy did so at monthly ministerial association meetings; some thought it was valuable, some did not. Topics discussed most frequently were Church unity, special Lenten services, welfare cases, common social problems, weeks of prayer, and shot-gun marriages. A mixed bag, but a fascinating one.

We knew that conversations between ourselves and other denominations were very frequent nowadays, but we wanted to discover how close our relationships were in certain sensitive fields. We wished to find out how our clergy felt in the area of Worship, always a touchy one, and we decided to test three points: helping with a Service, preaching a sermon, and celebrating Holy Communion.

We therefore asked: *Would you be in favor of a United Church minister or a Roman Catholic priest*:
> *Helping you with a Service?*
> *Preaching a Sermon?*
> *Celebrating Holy Communion?*

So far as helping with a service was concerned, 177 said *Yes* to United Church, 193 said *Yes* to Roman Catholic.

So far as preaching a Sermon was concerned, 183 said *Yes* to United Church, 202 to Roman Catholic.

So far as assisting in celebrating Holy Communion was concerned, 51 said *Yes* to United Church, 116 said *Yes* to Roman Catholic.

Eleven men said *No* to everything, and 5 left the question unanswered. Many pointed out that they would need the consent of their Church to do these things, but were otherwise in favor of them. Some others said that they would be in favor if there were careful preparation.

The most interesting response in the above was that which concerned celebrating Holy Communion with a United Church minister: 20% in favor.

So far as intercommunion is concerned, the matter is probably being solved long in advance of official declarations. There is still some uncertainty and coyness in the air, but a few unofficial inquiries (eighty people asked) made in the Diocese of Toronto reflects my own ten years' experience in Quebec—that intercommunion is very widely, even though unofficially, practised. Certainly a growing number of people move in and out of the Anglican, United and Presbyterian Churches without any obvious embarrassment and, given a freely conceded permission, many clergy might well do the same. The fact is that membership in a denomination indicates very little in terms of theology. In the Anglican Church alone we have long incorporated doctrines which cover almost every theological viewpoint. Some clergy feel more at home with their Roman Catholic friends than with some of their Anglican; others are more at home with the United Church.

Areas rather more difficult to interpret are those where there is, in the background, a theological difference of opinion which is only identified when some local prejudice brings it to light. One of the big divisions between ourselves and the 'Protestant' Churches lies in what is called our Doctrines of the Ministry. These doctrines are only significantly different at a very advanced level of theology. In his practice, an Anglican priest conducts his ministry in much the same way as a United Church minister. Taking into account the wide varieties of opinion in both Churches, it would be very difficult to state precisely where the difference lay.

In a local situation, therefore, Anglicans and United Churchmen can survive for a long time without any theological division. Sooner or later, however, as can be seen in many experiments with 'Joint Churches', a group of Anglicans discover that they ought to have a bishop for Confirmation. The implication is clear: they are stating (whatever the tactfulness of the wording) that they think a bishop is superior to a moderator or a minister. It is, therefore, not surprising that some of the United Church people find themselves driven into a strong denunciation of episcopacy. Nobody, however, really knows what the arguments for and against are; nor could the majority of the Anglicans give two acceptable reasons why a bishop is necessary. But, fired by local feelings, they will seek help and quickly find it. At that point, the advanced theological debate becomes a reality for them; and differences are identified and deepened.

It is for this reason that the theological niceties, though remote and absurd to outsiders and many insiders, are not unreal and are, at times, highly practical. One of the adjustments called for in the modern church, therefore, is one which is set before the theologians in university and seminary. In some ways, they must reconcile Anglican ideas with those of Rome on the one hand and the so-called Protestant denominations on the other. And they must hurry or it will be too late.

The resolution of theological differences is, however, only one step on the way. For, whatever may be decided at the levels of Archbishop and Moderator, the local churchman has to join forces with a group of people in his town or village. At this point, it is quickly discovered that the differences are not theological, but social. There are family histories to be considered, prejudices which arose, not when there was a difference over the doctrine of the sacraments, but when George had his stained glass window put in and Alex didn't like it. There are also the irritations which have nothing at all to do with anything important, but can still operate as major obstacles. The tunes used for hymns can be a great barrier and that barrier is increased when different denominations join together. John and Alice might find it easier to accept new doctrines than to sing the *Old Rugged Cross*.

Behind all this, there remains an old problem. A Rector in a north Toronto parish, preaching his new year sermon, stated that he did not expect reunion to come in 1965 because, deep in their hearts, people still felt they were better than others. When Bishop Bayne suggested that the Anglican Communion might one day cease to exist, not everyone approved his statement.* It is very difficult

---

*Some people misunderstood this, thinking he suggested the end of the Anglican Communion while everybody else remained as they were. He was, of course, implying the end of *all* denominations.

to sacrifice one's own little house to the Kingdom of God, and the reason is that we always feel our own house to be better than the other man's. Whatever brave sentiments we express about our 'brethren', they are still thought of as separated, slightly inferior, misguided, or even plain obstinate.

And all the time, pushing us back into our narrow prisons and trying to put God there, fear works its usual horrors. What, we think, will come of all this? At least we know where we stand at the moment. Perhaps—and this temptation will not always be resisted— the answer is to become more Anglican than ever before and make grander claims. Perhaps we are being disloyal to our forefathers when we indulge in this hobnobbing with what they used to call nonconformists. Perhaps we should draw the line now—before it is too late. If we go on like this, where will it all end? Shall we be left with nothing? Shall we, in our anxiety to feel at one with others, sacrifice our faith and everything we stand for?

The fears are legitimate and perhaps even necessary. Whenever we are willing to accept other people as equal with ourselves before God, we take a risk. It is a risk which Jesus constantly urged upon us. He who saves his life must lose it. He who protects his single talent will find even what he has taken from him. If we are ever going to find the Kingdom of God, we have to risk our whole Church life on the gamble. If we hold back anything, even the most precious little comforts of our worship or doctrine, we will place ourselves in the category of Ananias. We are not playing a card game in which we put as little as is possible to win; we are putting everything in because the Mission of the Church is to build the Kingdom of God and that Kingdom is based on Love and nothing less. And Love ceases to be Love at the point we hold something back, no matter how precious it may be.

Nonetheless, fears may still persist. Are we in danger of finishing up simply Unitarians? I don't think the label is of much importance here but the matter cannot be dismissed casually. There is always a trap set for us in any ecumenical effort—that of playing it safe. This quickly becomes a game in which we only discuss those matters which are comfortable and uncontroversial. Yet this is no way to work with other people. We don't find true love in a family because the members of it hide their real feelings from each other; we find true love when they share everything from admiration to hostility without finding barriers erected. So with different denominations.

The areas we need to discuss at any one moment are those where most heat is engendered, where emotions are highest, and where there is least mutual admiration. In practice, the safe approach happens too often and the results are predictable—wishy-washy, woolly decisions which fall to the ground under the first wind of opposition. Behind us is a long series of broken agreements which should never have been signed in the first place. For Unity does not come by pretending to be one, it comes when we know that the other person disagrees with us, that we do not like his ways, but that we recognize him as equal before God.

There is very little we can do separately any more. The minute we take a look at education, social work, or the mass media, we find the same result. Great effort and investment of time and talent are required—far greater than we can supply by ourselves. It is absurd that so much denominational work is merely duplicated from one Church to another. Much of what appears in educational curricula, training programs, stewardship programs, work amongst outcasts, and so on is common ground. In fact, in the present day world, only the most restricted philosopher could state where, in our practical work, we differ. We shall have to work together, or we shall not work at all.

The adjustments called for in the parish are, therefore, simple enough to state, though they will be difficult to practise. We have to consider the possibility that our theological differences are of another age, that they are no longer relevant, and that our theologians must rapidly work out a reconciliation. We shall have to be ready for the sacrifice, not only of major areas of philosophy (which is easy) but the little details (which is difficult). We shall, if we worship together, have to sing irritating tunes and join in irritating forms of prayer. We shall have to accept black gowns, surplices, or colored vestments as they come. We can still hang on to our own preferences, but we can learn not to let them influence our lives greatly. If there is to be one Church instead of two in our little town, we must be ready to accept the fact that our own may have to go*—the Church that has stood for a hundred years, where

---

*Local situations vary so widely that little more can be said. But it may be that the best solution to a problem where there are two vivid local traditions, both of which cannot be retained, is to jettison both and build from the ground up.

grandfather worshipped and gave the best years of his life as church-warden, where Bobby was baptized and the Christmas carol service has always been so beautiful. Yet, if we think of it, what are we sacrificing when compared with the sacrifices of those who were martyred or who, like Stringer and Ryerson, gave up a comfortable existence to struggle against the tyranny of nature and other men?

So far, in discussing our relationship with other denominations, I have been assuming that the adjustment required is the comparatively simple one of joining together those different Christian groups in which union is possible. But there is another question which needs raising.

The present division of the Church into denominations is a survival from the past which does not reflect the principal division in modern Christian thinking. I have taken part in innumerable discussions with different people. Unless we stumble across some revealing matter such as the Assumption of Mary or negative attitudes to alcohol, I can be in a group for hours before I have the least idea to which denomination the members belong. I often guess, but the guesses rarely prove accurate. But I know within a minute or so whether a person is looking back to some Golden Age of religion or forward to a Church which has passed through crisis into a new life.

This seems to be the modern division in Christendom. The two groups are found in all denominations. They set up the most marked split at the recent Vatican Council; they are to be found in the Anglican, United and Presbyterian Churches in all countries. They are to be found in society at large. They are both substantial and they both include enthusiastic members. Neither has the victory in debate or in conviction, loyalty, and faith.

If this is, in fact, the new division in the church, then we may take hope. For, if the organizational structure of the Church—now heavily weighted in favor of the Conservative element—is modified to enable the voice of others to be heard, and decisions to take note of their views, then there will be no schism along these lines. And, if it is the chief division, it will soon enable us to see our denominations as the nonsense they really are.

CHAPTER TWELVE

OTHER RELIGIONS

We now come to the position into which God is guiding us towards the end of our century. So far, I have described in this book some of the stages by which man has acknowledged the fact that God goes free. Our past attempts at tying him down have proved futile, but each new discovery of God's freedom has produced pain for the discoverers. It was not easy for our ancestors to realize that God could not be tied inside a box: that he would not be restricted to the words of patriarchs, kings, or prophets; and that he refused to be a prisoner within a single race, even the race he had chosen. Yet God's will prevailed and the old boxes fell into pieces.

During the past few centuries, we have been making new discoveries which are still as painful as the old ones and which have not yet been fully accepted. It is not easy for us to realize that God will not be held a prisoner within a single Church, denomination or sect; that he refuses to tie himself inside a Bible, a Creed or a Catechism; that he escapes from Prayer Books, Liturgies and Rituals; and that the institution known as the Anglican Church will, as Bishop Bayne warned us, end.

It is particularly painful to move in God's freedom because we are afraid. And, in our fear, we set ourselves up as exclusively right. It is very comforting to feel that we have the correct answers, the true faith, and the pure morality whereas the other man is in error, faithlessness, and immorality. Yet we have to come to terms with Jesus' constant warning that we are not to judge. Physician, heal thyself.

The next hill which we have to climb lies ahead of us, although some people have trodden the first foothills. The shrinking of the modern world has not only brought us all into intimate contact, through television and movies, with other peoples; it has brought us into a confrontation with other religions. In the past, there was no reason to consider this as important. Our knowledge of other religions was minimal and their beliefs could be dismissed as inferior, superstitious, or heathen. We never bothered to check because the other religions never made it necessary. They were, for the most part, held by races and tribes who were kept in a state of subservience and even slavery by the white Christian races.

With political freedom has come a desire to speak out openly. This always happens when serfs, slaves and underlings find freedom. It is an irony that the overseer or the boss is only dealt with firmly and harshly when in fact he has given some measure of freedom to his underlings. So long as he holds the whip and denies any freedoms, he can remain in charge; he will find few rebellions, and those pointless.

Sooner or later, however, the human being finds himself driven by God's freedom. It is only for a limited period of time that one nation can enslave another. Eventually there comes a moment when the controlling race feels compunction, pity and a need to give the servants their freedom. And the first reaction of the freed slave, once he has adjusted to the fact, is to bite the hand that freed him. This is important and must always be recognized as important by the person who gives freedom. It was certainly recognized by God, who found that man did the same thing.

After the slave has freed himself from his master, he eventually enters on the long process of freeing himself from his old ideas; and this happens especially in his religion. It is no accident that the freeing of India led so quickly to a revival of India's religions.

These religions are now at our doorsteps and will soon enter our houses and become equal with us. What, at this point, will we do?

I remember talking with a Roman Catholic priest who had been on a prolonged tour of the middle east about five years ago. No longer, he said, could we think in terms of converting people to our own point of view simply because we had a superior faith or religion. We must learn to live alongside them, helping where possible. Their religion was a thing which could only earn admiration. The conversation took me back to 1947 when my wife and I were talking with the Church Missionary Society about the possibility of going to Pakistan. Even then, it was made clear to us that we could go simply because, as Christians, it was necessary to help others in their clear need. The possibilities of 'evangelization' in the Victorian sense—that of winning people over to a so-called Christian point of view—were listed by Dr. Harold Anderson as nil. The attitude was that of the Peace Corps, a modern missionary movement. The same point comes to life vividly in John Taylor's *Primal Vision*: 'As the Christian meets the pagan and attempts to proclaim Christ, is it a simple case of either-or? . . . Ruthlessness has had a long run in Africa, and so long as the missionary encounter is conceived of as a dialogue, one will have to "cede to the other". But may it not be truer to see it as a meeting of three, in which Christ has drawn together the witness who proclaims him and the other who does not know his name, so that in their slow discovery of one another each may discover more of him?'

We are once again reminded of the Parable of the Sheep and the Goats. Christ is to be found in areas where his name has never been heard and is often absent in areas which call constantly upon him. Not every one that saith unto me Lord, Lord, shall enter the kingdom of Heaven. Yet, whenever men come together, in any context, for the purpose of seeing themselves and the others clearly, then Christ is present. No man can come unto the Father except by me, said Jesus. Therefore, whenever we find God, it must be through Jesus, whether we know it or not, whether we say Creeds or not, whether we utter loud cries of Lord Lord, or not. The test is not the outward words or even the outward thoughts, but the inward reality of each man, which God alone is able to judge.

As soon as we think of living alongside other religions in a spirit of mutual acceptance and interdependence, we find the old fears raising their heads. Are we in danger of selling the gospel down the river? If God saves everybody, why bother to do anything about it? If the Christian religion is not superior to others, and my life not better than that of the atheist, why the effort? Why not simply sit back and leave it to God?

The answer to this is that the fears are groundless. When I discover more about a Jew, a Muslim, a Buddhist, or a Hindu, I finish up with more than I started. I know more of God and so does he. Moreover, whether I like it or not, I have to live. I have to discover myself. And it is easily seen that I cannot discover myself in isolation from others. Unless I escape to the top of a pole and am forgotten (surely an impossibility these days), I am bound up in the whole of mankind. And every time I make a new discovery about myself and others, I am making a discovery about God. It is through his people that Christ works and his people are those who do the will of God. This will is often done in and through the Christian Church, but is not limited to the Christian Church.

We are often in the habit of sitting down with a member of another Faith and making it clear that we think we have more of the truth than he has and that he will find God more quickly if he will join us. When we do this, we chop God out of the discussion, ironically enough in the name of God himself. It may truly be said that many people have been driven from Christ by those who noisily proclaim themselves his followers.

George Lewis, in an article headed *You Are the Church—Therefore Be the Church*, challenges us to say what we mean by Mission. It is a big word these days and this book you are reading is written for Anglican World Mission. But what do we mean by it? I think I have been trying to imply an answer throughout these chapters, and George Lewis raises the question which lies at the heart of everything we do today. What, he asks, is the job of the Church in the world? We are concerned with great machinery, both in parish and diocese. What is it for? His answer is not presented as the only possible one, but it is: to extend God's Kingdom throughout the world. 'If,' he writes, 'as the evangelist says, "God is love," then clearly it is the Kingdom of Love which is to be brought first into all areas of our own lives, for only then can it be extended through us to all parts of the one world in which we live. A large order? Yes, a very large order indeed! . . . This briefly is what is meant by mission—*the extension of God's Kingdom of Love.*'

I think that Mr. Lewis' description is helpful because, as soon as we ask how this Kingdom is to be perceived, we find that he has made it possible to follow Jesus and see that those under his rule vary widely in style, spirit, theology, and morality. A Kingdom does not consist of people, all of whom say, think and act in the same manner. God's Kingdom does not even exclude those who are unaware of the ruler. If there is Love, then the ruler is there, no matter what words are spoken.

Moreover, Mr. Lewis' description makes us realize that Mission is not concerned with 'overseas' except insofar as overseas is part of the world, and therefore part of God's Kingdom. 'A visiting missionary,' he says, 'recently made the disturbing point that "in the mission field, denominationalism is suicidal to the Christian cause." Perhaps this fact does not disturb us as it should—until we realize that we ourselves are living in the midst of a rapidly growing mission field.' This is well said. The Kingdom of God is established where there is Love, and geography has very little to do with it.

The situation which meets us in the modern world is that we are in continual contact with other religions, whether we are at home or overseas. And these other religions include, not only such clear-cut examples as Hinduism and Buddhism, but also agnosticism, communism and so forth. They are all, in a variety of ways, trying to establish their respective Kingdoms, and the fundamental test which the Christian needs to apply is whether the Kingdom is built upon Love. If it is, then it may be accepted and supported in whatever way seems appropriate. In doing this, there is no surrender of the love which Christ inspires in us and which was so clearly exemplified by his life. Only when the Kingdom which is being established is built upon Hate or anti-Love have we the right or duty to regard the other religion as one to be vigorously opposed and attacked.

What is the adjustment which we are called upon to make? It is that we no longer regard those who are non-Christian as if they were opposed to the Kingdom of God. We must learn to co-exist with them.

We can, in the first place, find out enough of what the other religions stand for to convince us that they are deeply seeking the things of God. There is no need to find out everything, nor even a massive amount. It takes most of us a lifetime to come within any understanding of the variety and depth of Jesus' message, let alone those of others. But even a glance at the faiths of other peoples and races quickly convinces us that we are dealing with something substantial, far from the 'heathen' or 'pagan' labels imposed on them by previous generations.*

We need not simply accept this as a sad fact of the modern world;

---

*There are many good books which help us. The best I know is also one of the shortest: *World Religions* by Helen Milton, a pamphlet which is only 71 pages long, and which may be secured from the Anglican Book Centre, 600 Jarvis Street, Toronto 5, Ont. It deals with God and the great Religions, Hindus and Hinduism, Buddhists and the Buddha, Judaism and the Jews, Christians and the Christ, and Islam and the Muslims.

we can be glad of the new situation. In his Congress address, John Lawrence said: 'We live in a secular age; and we ought to welcome secularization, for it gives us opportunities which were denied to previous generations of Christians. Let me explain. At one time religion was a very large department of life, but it was still only one department and the relation of the Christian faith to most of the hours of the day in the lives of most Christians was marginal; and nothing wrong was seen in this . . . It was possible for a devout churchman to employ child labour for cruel hours at a starvation wage, or even to engage in the slave trade without thinking that religion had anything to do with the business, so long as he traded honestly. Then the secular world began to encroach on the religious department of life.'

What he said of the secularization of modern life can be extended to include the encroachment of other religions—resurging, re-vitalized, strong religions, also facing their own secularization. In the old days, it was possible to be a Christian and enslave others. Now we have to live alongside them as brothers. This is surely a matter for gladness, even though it causes us some difficulty in our attitudes and our medieval-type theology.

Moreover, it leads us for the first time in Christian history since the Emperor Constantine to the road known as humility. It is a tricky road and often vanishes when we start talking about it; but we can no longer go to others as 'top dogs'. I am inclined to think that we cannot even go as equals any more. For, with their background of association with western imperialism, Christians may have less to offer than some others to the modern world, which is a black and yellow world. 'Our first task,' says Max Warren, 'in approaching another people, another culture, another religion, is to take off our shoes, for the place we are approaching is holy. Else we may find ourselves treading on men's dreams. More serious still, we may forget that God was here before our arrival. We have to ask what is the authentic religious content in the experience of the Muslim, the Buddhist or whoever he may be. We may, if we have asked humbly and respectfully, still reach the conclusion that our brothers have started from a false premise and reached a faulty conclusion. But we must not arrive at our judgement from outside their religious situation. We have to try to sit where they sit . . . We have, in a word, to be "present" with them.'

And so we reach the end of the trail, a few small points of which have been mapped out in previous pages. We have seen how, in successive generations, men have expanded the areas in which God is seen to work. Prison after prison has had its gates opened and God has been seen to go free, each new freedom bringing man closer to his Creator. At each moment of new freedom, there have been many who have protested loudly, bewailing the decline of what they call the 'old, true religion'. Yet, though there have been long and severe setbacks, the freedoms have remained.

The biggest gate to be opened, for Christians, was the coming of Christ, which was also met with great cries of anguish, protest, and the need to kill. During the past century, more areas than ever have been proved to be filled with the Spirit of God. He has been seen to transcend our Church, our Creeds, and now, as we move to the end of the century, we can see that there are no limits at all to be set. We can see him, and be glad to see him, at work everywhere in the creation which, after all, is his.

CHAPTER THIRTEEN

WHAT'S IN IT FOR ME?

We have examined some areas of life where the Church is being challenged by modern society, both by outsiders and its own members. The implication throughout has been that we must examine these challenges carefully and adjust to their presence.

They need not all be accepted as legitimate, certainly not simply because they are modern; for modern science, technology and theology can become prisons just as much as the old ones were. There will be some modern ideas which will vanish like froth; some which will linger for a while and depart from our scene; and some which will survive, bear fruit and become built into our Faith. Christianity is described in the New Testament as 'The Way' and a Way demands movement. To stand still on a road makes it useless. God did not stop creating in the days of the Law, the Bible, the early Church, the Creed, the medieval scholars, the Reformation, the revivalist period, the Oxford Movement, Bonhoeffer, or you and me. He is continually creating and this continual creation means change. The problem for us lies in perceiving which changes are to be welcomed, which accepted and tolerated, and which rejected.

Whatever the changes may be, however, they will ultimately have some practical effect in everyday Church life, which is presently reflected for the most part in the Parish and Diocese. What sort of adjustments are called for in the Parishes of the future? Can they be made? Can they be made in time?

Here are a few suggestions for consideration. They cannot all be implemented at once and some of them may not be implemented at all.

1. We must take a very close look at our parish, diocesan and national church organizations. In the December 1964 issue of *Parish and People* the Editor, with the Church of England in mind, writes:

73

'The Church Assembly should initiate a root and branch reform of the structure of the Church's governmental life at national and diocesan levels . . . The reform of the electoral system of the Church Assembly and the holding of its meetings at weekends so that ordinary men and women can attend is an obvious necessity. If the Church is ever to come to terms with its mission in the twentieth century it needs genuine lay insights at every level of its life. It is sheer folly to entrust the central government of the Church to the "squires from the shires and the spinsters from the spas," and there can be no excuse for allowing the present arrangements to continue.'

This could be as accurately said of the Canadian Church, whose Synods—national, provincial, and diocesan—are built on a Victorian concept of society in which the Church was expected to be run by bishops and clergy, assisted by lawyers, bankers, retired colonels and people of private means. To hold General Synods, as we do, during the week, is to fall into the trap outlined above, for it is only a small segment of society that can get away from work on weekdays. The results are obvious to anyone who attends General Synods or the meetings of Executive Council; they are dominated by people from the privileged classes of society.

At the diocesan level, it is not so easy to analyse, because Canada is very varied. The larger dioceses, however, suffer from the English malaise. In the above article, the editor might almost be describing the Synods of such dioceses:'Visitors to Diocesan Conferences (the English Synods) know that they are rarely diocesan and never conferences. The combination of unwieldly size and episcopal control turns most of them into second-rate lecture societies.' In most large Canadian dioceses it is almost impossible for anything but the approved matters of the Executive to find their way on to the floor of Synod and, when they do, those in control have quick ways of squelching them.

At the parish level, representation is better, but there is a tendency to allow the Rector and Churchwardens to dictate the flow of vestry and other meetings. This is by no means universal, and the only suggestion made here is that those parishes which have fallen into the habit of leaving it to the clergy and 'Board', ask themselves if it is time to stop the practice. They may find that authoritarian rule is prescribed, or implied by diocesan Canons. If that turns out to be the case, then a clamor may well be made for a root and branch revision of the Canons to bring them into modern life. The motto should be the same as Jesus offered us in connection with the Sabbath: 'The Canons were made for the parishioner, not the parishioner for the Canons.'

2. Stewardship is a key to change. I am not thinking here of the development of good stewardship in our private incomes, because adjustment is taking place, even though slowly. I am thinking rather of the bad stewardship which we have allowed to creep on us. We are always lecturing other people in society on the waste and self-indulgence which are typical of modern life; we rarely stop to challenge our own use of Church resources. *Parish and People* once more shows us where English life and Canadian are identical. 'There are few points of the country in which thousands of pounds and man-hours are not being squandered on the maintenance of redundant buildings and obsolete units of parochial life. The mission of the Church is being stifled by the incessant demands of maintenance.'

This is well said. There are parishes right across Canada which are unable to function because their total energies are dedicated to paying off the mortgages imposed on them by past congregations. Nor is there much sign of a changed attitude to this irresponsibility. There are new areas around many large cities where a disastrous building program need not be undertaken but where, it is abundantly clear, it will be. Once again the mission will be sacrificed to a building.

In a brilliant book called *The Local Church*, John Lee* sums this up:

'The local church is also involved in a race for institutional success. This may be a valuable goal, but the pressures it puts upon the local church are anything but salutary. The local church is judged by the size of its budget and the number of its members. The hallmark of such success is a new building. . . . In the words of at least one United Appeal planner, in comparison with campaigns for community welfare, "the Churches have got it made".

A New Look at the Local Church, John R. Lee. Published by the Ryerson Press in co-operation with the Anglican Church of Canada and the Presbyterian Church.

Who, even among the skeptical, would doubt the necessity of sacred buildings prominent in place in the community, as monuments to our devotion and our piety? One need only look at the billions of dollars spent in North America on church construction in any one year, to get proof that people will part with more money more readily for buildings than for the Christian mission in our own land or in other lands. The expectation is that a building there must be. The first pristine days of life of many a local congregation have been one long round of bazaars, teas, fashion shows and campaigns to pay off the mortgage. A far cry from the Book of Acts and the Church in apostolic times.

'A popular minister, brand new buildings, well-attended services, a high "level of giving", these are the marks of ecclesiastical success. But they are simply the marks of secular success transferred to the Church by the world . . . This is secularization in the worst sense. The world which does not acknowledge Jesus as Lord is allowed to dictate to the Church the terms upon which it may succeed or fail. Church extension, the building of new local churches, is too often a clear case of the Church extending *itself*. Our denomination must have churches in every new residential area. The mission of the denomination is thought of as some kind of chaplaincy to its members. There seems to be no thought that the Church exists for those who do not belong to it. . . . There are thousands of Churches in Canada now, and hundreds more building every year. It would be a betrayal of Christian devotion to write them off as white elephants, or to damn them with the faint praise that they have a valid, but limited, ministry. Is it, perhaps, unrealistic to ask if we could hold up the building of any more until we decide what they are really for.'

I have quoted this at length because it seems to me to strike right to the heart of modern parochial work. If you are contemplating a new church, ask yourself why? Is it necessary? What do you hope to accomplish in building it? What is the work of the Church where you live? Could the mission be carried out in other ways?

Once you ask these fundamental questions about the parish— what it is for and whether it is organized best to carry on its work in the middle of the twentieth century—you are coming to terms with the Gospel of Christ. The conclusions may be startling, they may not. You may find, for example, that it is absurd to build a church hall when there are many other buildings in the district which you could use or rent. You may find that it is foolish to set up rooms on church premises when the local Y.M.C.A. is running study groups and where Bible study (for example) could be conducted in a multi-denominational atmosphere.

But these are only suggestions, and some of them may be irrelevant to your local situation. The common element is that the Parish demand of itself what it is trying to do and refuse to build a local building (no matter how much pressure comes from the Diocese) until it has decided why, and whether the cost of building it is too great in terms of those parts of the work which may be neglected as a result of acquiring a heavy mortgage.

3. In Chapter Two, I raised the question of the relationship between clergy and laity. It is now possible to suggest to you this question: is the Parish the best medium for modern mission? There can be no question that it was ideal in days when communities lived together for generation after generation. But is it ideal today? Or even useful? Modern man lives in many societies and only one of these is the society in which he sleeps. Yet we gear most of our expensive efforts to dealing with this one area. It is important, of course, and I am not suggesting that the Parish is redundant. It is, however, only one area of work and should be considered only as one area. Others are equally important, some of them perhaps more important.

The Roman Catholic Church is far ahead of us in these matters. Already they have fewer men engaged in the parish ministry than outside of it in all settled areas of Canada. In one large Diocese in a thickly populated part of the country, plans have now been made for a massive reconstruction. No longer is the Diocese to be thought of in geographical terms, but in functional terms. There will be one 'zone' to deal with the dormitory and family work (the present parochial system), one to deal with Trade Union matters, one with educational matters, one with business affairs, one with broken marriages, and so forth. The details have not yet been made precise, but the principle is clear and it is one which we too should examine.

Now, if the Church is to move outside itself and work with the general population, it will not be allowed to do so in any narrow denominational manner. In the Church of the near future, there will have to be large numbers of clergy who never talk about Anglicanism or the Prayer Book or even churchgoing at all. At the moment, the few who are engaged in the sharpest Christian mission feel lonely. They are scarcely recognized by colleagues and almost never by the hierarchy. Those who have gone into schoolteaching or insurance work are considered as having 'left the ministry'. But what could such a phrase possibly mean? How can a schoolteacher, or a doctor, or an insurance agent be said to have left the ministry so long as he is a human being and a member of Christ? How can he be said to have left the ministry if he is engaged in any work of reconciliation, healing, or acceptance?

Here then, is an adjustment which can quickly be made. Let the clergy move in and out of parish work with freedom. A man is a priest whatever his daily work may be. There is nothing specially Christian about pottering around a parish, nor unChristian for that matter. It is simply one way of working in the modern world. Our error has been to try to imprison the whole Mission in that one area, as if parish work were the only possible ministry open to a parson.

This will mean that you have to adjust financially. Some of your money may well go on your own congregation and its well-being. But much of it will be for paying the stipend of a clergyman you may never see in your church. He may be overseas, he may be in the factory round the corner. But you will be a partner with him in the Mission of the Church, which is what this book has been about.